Orange Appeal

SAVORY and SWEET

JAMIE SCHLER

Photographs by ILVA BERETTA

GIBBS SMITH
TO ENRICH AND INSPIRE HUMANKIND

First Edition
21 20 19 18 17   5 4 3 2 1

Text © 2017 Jamie Schler
Photographs © 2017 Ilva Beretta

Published by
Gibbs Smith
P.O. Box 667
Layton, Utah 84041

1.800.835.4993 orders
www.gibbs-smith.com

Designed by Rita Sowins / Sowins Design
Printed and bound in Hong Kong

Gibbs Smith books are printed on either recycled, 100% post-consumer waste, FSC-certified pa-
pers or on paper produced from sustainable PEFC-certified forest/controlled wood source. Learn
more at www.pefc.org.

Library of Congress Cataloging-in-Publication Data

Names: Schler, Jamie.
Title: Orange appeal : savory and sweet / Jamie Schler ; photographs by
Ilva Beretta.
Description: First edition. | Layton, Utah : Gibbs Smith, 2017. |
Includes index.
Identifiers: LCCN 2017000514 | ISBN 9781423646693 (hardcover)
Subjects: LCSH: Cooking (Oranges) | LCGFT: Cookbooks.
Classification: LCC TX813.O6 S35 2017 | DDC 641.6/431--dc23 LC record
available at https://lccn.loc.gov/2017000514

To my father, Morton,
        my brother, Michael,
and my husband, Jean-Pierre,
    the men who, with love
and patience, taught me how
to cook.

Contents

Introduction

"A day without orange juice is like
a day without sunshine."

What was a simple tagline, a snappy television
jingle for a fruit juice commercial became a
familiar, emblematic tune that shaped the culture
of my youth.

I grew up on Florida's Space Coast, the narrow ribbon of land sandwiched between the Atlantic Ocean and the Banana and Indian Rivers, stretching from Cape Canaveral down to Sebastian Inlet. This area is well known for its surfing and boating, its long stretch of sandy white beaches, *I Dream of Jeannie,* and the Space Program.

Yet this slice of the Sunshine State I call home has long suffered the reputation of being an urban environment immersed in a hot, humid, hostile landscape that gives no hint of having any kind of culinary value. Florida's natural flora is wild, harsh, and savage—a profusion of thick-leaved spiky plants, prickly scrub, and itchy lawns hiding stickers that bite into your feet, and burning sand in a survival-of-the-fittest battle with all things green. It is easy to think that nothing sweet and luscious could possibly be hidden beneath all the anger.

But growing up in Florida, we were taught from an early age that the waters and the land proffered a bounty of succulent gifts. Locals know, and visitors quickly learn, that the area's food culture, outdoorsy and casual, is incredibly rich with fish and seafood, the waters generous with bass, flounder and snapper, shrimp, blue crab, oysters, squid, octopus, spiny lobster, conch, and alligator. The Florida climate is ideal for a wide variety of hardy fruit plants and trees—peaches, mangos, avocados, tomatoes, watermelons, and sweet juicy strawberries are indigenous to the region—nurtured by the temperate, subtropical climate, and growing in abundance. And anyone who is familiar with this stretch of central Florida knows the Indian River and knows that on the Space Coast of Florida, citrus is king!

I spent my youth a stone's throw from the orchards that line the Indian River—world renowned for its grapefruits, tangerines, and oranges—and winter was always reserved for citrus. I waited impatiently all hot, lazy summer long through the equally hot but busy fall for winter, when the

citrus ritual began all over again, the same as the year before and every year for as long as I can remember. Saturday trips in the station wagon to the citrus groves on the other side of the river just over the bridge rewarded us with brown paper grocery bags bursting with citrus—ruby reds or white grapefruits, tangelos, Valencias, Honeybells, Temples, navels, and tangerines. Once back home, Dad would line the bags up on the workbench in the cool garage where they would sit all throughout the winter until the end of the season; the bags refilled as fast as we could devour the contents.

I would dash out into the chilly garage and dip into one of the crinkly brown paper bags to fish out a few tangerines or an orange or two then dash back into the warmth of the house. We kids would simply peel the fruit and eat the segments, nothing fancy, just orange after orange until the last bag of the season was empty. When a trip to the groves wasn't convenient, my parents would stop by one of the many fruit stands minutes from the house and grab a huge mesh bag or two stuffed with fresh oranges. We were never without citrus.

Once or twice during the season, we would head to the groves with the Girl Scouts, our youth group, or a school club to pick oranges in the winter sunshine, some to eat, most to sell to raise money for charity or a school trip. Harvey's, Hale's, and Indian River Fruit are names that still stick with me, their logos still familiar.

It's little wonder that the Florida Citrus Commission selected the orange as its hero and mascot, bypassing the just-this-side-of-bitter grapefruit, tart lemons, and tangy tangerines in favor of the sweet orange orb, forever connecting the fruit to the state with its "Come to the Florida Sunshine Tree! Florida sunshine naturally!" against a logo of an orange tree. Oranges were first planted in what is now northern Florida in the mid-sixteenth century by Spanish explorers, possibly Ponce de Leon, and were first cultivated commercially in the Sunshine State at the end of the eighteenth century, the area's tropical climate and soil making it the ideal location for growing citrus.

Today, Florida is one of the world's largest producers of oranges; in 2011–2012 Florida accounted for sixty-five percent of total US citrus production. But the Indian River is particularly known for cultivating incredibly sweet oranges yielding very high quality juice, as those TV commercials testify, and Brazil and Florida combined make up approximately eighty-five percent of the world's production of orange juice. No wonder oranges are part of my culture, growing up so close to a tremendous concentration of groves producing world-class, world-famous fruit.

Living in Florida, my parents received slews of thin pamphlets and brochures from one or another of the citrus growers' associations or commissions urging the consumption of local citrus, tempting home cooks with recipes from Florida chefs or inspired by local cuisines, pairing oranges, tangerines, and grapefruits with Florida's fresh fish and seafood, layered in salads or gelatin molds, the juice flavoring muffins, cakes, and soufflés.

Rarely, though, did citrus find its way into our kitchen other than sliced or peeled and pulled apart into sections, or juiced. My parents never considered baking a soufflé or a cake with oranges, and we kids didn't have the patience to wait or the desire to taste anything but the pure, unadulterated fruit. I left Florida a long time ago, moving north for university and then to Europe, but the craving for oranges come the first hint of cool autumn weather, the harbinger of orange season, has stuck with me; I think that I have orange juice running through my veins.

Yet while oranges were strictly for eating *as is* when I was a child, as an adult and now a passionate cook and baker, while I still eat one or two a day (for my much-needed allotment of sunshine!), I find myself increasingly using the juice and the zest and the fruit in chunks, segments, or slices in baking and for cooking, always searching for and developing new recipes.

When oranges are scarce (and even when they aren't), I find myself stirring spoonfuls of marmalade, sweet or bitter, into cake and brownie batters, sauces, or marinades. Orange powder, extracts or liqueurs, Grand Marnier, Cointreau, and Triple Sec, or delicate orange blossom water add the orange essence to a dish or pastry, whether accentuating or replacing the fresh fruit, zest, or its juice. Our favorite dishes and desserts, like panna cotta, rice pudding, and sponge cakes, are all transformed by the flavor of orange.

Over the years, I have discovered that the orange is extremely well adapted to both sweet and savory dishes. The orange embraces and creates a wonderful working relationship with spices on both ends of the spectrum—bold and delicate—from cumin, coriander, chili, and saffron to the warm spices most commonly used in baking and pastry, such as cinnamon, nutmeg, clove, ginger, allspice, pumpkin pie, or gingerbread spices. Oranges pair well with many fresh herbs like mint, rosemary, sage, basil, thyme, fresh coriander, or cilantro.

The orange marries beautifully with fish and seafood, of course, but also poultry, lamb, pork, veal, and beef. Sweet potatoes and squash varieties, pumpkin, beets, jicama, fennel, Belgian endive, kale, and carrots all benefit from the orange. A wide variety of fruits and berries—cranberries, blueberries and cherries, strawberries, persimmon, pineapple, figs, and grapes—nuts—walnuts, pecans, hazelnuts, and almonds in particular—and of course, chocolate or vanilla all balance beautifully with orange, each flavor accentuated by and accenting the other exquisitely. And don't forget how well orange goes with wine, rum, brandy, bourbon, and whiskey!

In short, oranges go with just about everything, thus making them an extraordinary and indispensable ingredient, a versatile and remarkable flavoring in the kitchen. Whether the flavor shines boldly through, the fruit the star of the show, or whether the addition of the juice or zest of an orange subtly alters the overall flavor effect of the combination of ingredients—adding sweetness or warmth, taming bitterness, tartness, saltiness, or heat—the addition of the fruit, juice, or zest brings an astonishing taste metamorphosis to soups and salads, dressings, sauces, marinades and glazes, and baked goods and desserts.

Growing up as I did and where I did, my desire for oranges is practically innate. It is part of my culture and part of my being, and this collection of recipes came so naturally. But it is not meant to be the definitive book on all things *oranges*. In fact, I rarely recommend one variety of orange over another, instead encouraging you to use whatever you find in your local market or even a mix of varieties. Rather, I hope to inspire home cooks of all levels of expertise and experience, no matter where in the country or in the world you live, to cook and bake with oranges, to discover the extraordinary transformation the simple orange will bring to a dish.

I wanted to bring together a collection of recipes that reflect my kitchen, how I cook and bake for my family and friends. So I have created recipes that are simple and quick to execute, homey and comforting, pleasing all tastes, but always with a definite *wow* factor. I have also included a few recipes for those times when you, like I sometimes do, have a long, lazy day ahead of you, possess the energy and desire to knead dough, or stir soup, try something new, create something a bit more complex and time consuming. Several of the recipes reflect my multicultural home and kitchen with traditional French, Italian, and Moroccan dishes, as well as a few with Indian or Middle Eastern flair. I hope to offer you recipes that will find their way into your own repertoire of dishes that you make for your family and friends over and over again.

I have lived in big cities, small towns, and villages. I have lived in the United States, in Italy, and now in France, and I carry my favorite recipes and cookbook collection wherever I move to. I know the struggle to adapt recipes, to search for unusual, exotic ingredients or appropriate substitutes, or find something that just isn't common to where I currently live, so most of my recipes use easy-to-find ingredients most everywhere, often pantry staples, keeping each dish and dessert accessible to all.

Orange Varieties

Although I love lemons, limes, and grapefruit, I consider the orange the most versatile of the citrus family—sweet, tart, sour, or bitter varieties offering infinite possibilities in the kitchen. The orange offers the fruit or flesh itself, but also the rind, zest, and juice, ideally serving as feature ingredient or a simple flavoring—an incredibly multifaceted and complete kitchen staple. Like any fruit, the orange is a huge dietary plus, but most people simply associate the orange with its content of vitamin C. Yet oranges are fat and sodium free, have only about sixty to seventy calories each (one cup of juice is about 120 calories), and are a great source of fiber. Oranges are a rich source of vitamin C, yes, but also vitamins A, E, B (including B1), as well as potassium, calcium, copper, phosphorus, niacin, folic acid, folate, and magnesium. So not only are oranges versatile and delicious, they contain more health benefits than many people realize. And because oranges are indigenous to so many countries and regions of the world, they can be found in dishes and as a flavoring in a multitude of cuisines, and are quite possibly one of the most common and universal of ingredients.

Oranges can be divided into three categories: sweet oranges (often divided into common/juice and navel/eating or table oranges), bitter or sour oranges, and blood oranges. Although winter is traditionally orange season, you can now find one variety or another of sweet orange, juice, or navel orange on the market all year round. Bitter oranges and blood oranges are rarer, usually available only in the winter.

SWEET ORANGE VARIETIES

COMMON SWEET OR JUICE ORANGE VARIETIES

Common sweet or juice oranges are most frequently used for their juice and grow best in subtropical, temperate regions, with warm and sunny days, cooler nights, hot summers, and chilly winters allowing for optimal color, sweetness, and flavor development. Common or juice oranges differ from many navel varieties by being smaller, thinner-skinned, a bit more difficult to peel, and producing more juice. But for cooking or baking, as far as I'm concerned, juice and navel oranges are interchangeable as long as they are fresh and sweet.

The most common varieties of juice oranges include: Ambersweet, a medium-size seedy, easy-to-peel orange with a tangerine flavor; Hamlin, a thin-skinned, easy-to-peel, mostly seedless, very sweet orange with little tartness; the very sweet but delicate, larger Pineapple orange; Temple, a flavorful and fragrant medium-size easy-to-peel table orange; the sweet, juicy Parson Brown, another orange with a lot of seeds and thick skin; and Valencia, the most popular and widely commercialized orange in the world, often called "The King of Juice Oranges," which is thin-skinned, very sweet and juicy, and has few seeds. The Valencia are great eating and juice oranges and can often be found long after the other varieties are no longer in season, often well into the summer, sometimes running into autumn. Yellow or "blonde" Maltese/Malta or *Maltaise,* sweet juice oranges found in North Africa and Europe, are often used to make marmalade and are great for cooking. Satsuma are Mandarin oranges and considered one of the sweetest, most aromatic orange varieties, seedless, with a thin, loose, bumpy rind that peels easily, most often used in salads or jams rather than cooking or baking. The Jaffa, or Shamouti, orange was developed in Israel and now grows across the Middle East, Europe, and Florida, and is a very sweet orange with thick rind. The Florida Jaffa is a small to medium-size fruit with a thin, smooth peel, very tender flesh, and very sweet nectar-like juice.

NAVEL ORANGE VARIETIES

Navels and navelinas are also common sweet oranges but are more often considered eating or table oranges than ideal juicers or for cooking and baking, primarily because of their sweetness with a touch of tartness, their thicker, easy-to-peel skin, and segments that are a cinch to pull apart and more toothsome than juicy orange segments. Navels, so called for their familiar "belly buttons" on the blossom end, opposite the stem end, are very sweet and flavorful with few, if any, seeds, making them a favorite in my kitchen. Navelinas have all the characteristics of navels, but where navels tend to be large to extra-large oranges, navelinas are medium to medium-large. They are also widely available, so if you can't find juice oranges, do not hesitate to grab navels for cooking and baking.

Common varieties include: Cara Cara, a juicy, very sweet, sometimes mildly tart orange with a distinctive hint of berries (the Cara Cara, a medium-size fruit smaller than many navel varieties, is seedless, and the flesh runs the gamut from pale pink, to pink-orange, to a deeper pink-red—when it can be called Red Navel. It is ideal for baking, both savory and sweet salads, and desserts, and is especially pretty when layered with orange oranges and redder blood oranges); Lane Late (summer navel) or Navel Late are very juicy with a fine pulp; Fukumoto is a medium-size seedless, early maturing variety that is sweet, juicy, and rich in flavor with a reddish-orange rind; Bahia, Washington, or Riverside navels or navelinas are extremely common (or simply find oranges labeled navel or navelina).

BITTER OR SOUR ORANGE VARIETIES

Bitter or sour oranges are just that; not only is the rind bitter, but the flesh and the juice can be from very tart or acidic to sour to extremely bitter. These varieties appear briefly on the market in winter and are primarily used to make marmalade, but a squeeze of bitter orange juice in sauces or vinaigrettes alongside sweet orange juice adds an intriguing complexity and flavor. Bitter oranges can be recognized by their thick, sometimes loose, bumpy peel and have many seeds. The peel is excellent for making candied peel and is used to make orange liqueurs such as Cointreau, Grand Marnier, and Triple Sec. A strip of the zest is very flavorful and will add a zing to tea or infusions.

The Seville or Bigarade orange, the most well-known of the bitter oranges, has a thick and bumpy or dimpled rind, is very high in pectin—higher than sweet oranges—and is the most common orange used for bitter marmalade. The juice of the Seville can add complexity to a citrus tart, cream, ice cream or sorbet, or sauce when blended with other citrus such as limes or sweet oranges. These bitter oranges are also used to makes syrups, sauces, and orange wine. Their flowers are used to make orange blossom or orange flower water. The Bergamot orange, grown primarily in Italy, is rarer than the Seville and is used to make oil and as a flavoring in Earl Grey tea.

BLOOD ORANGE VARIETIES

Blood oranges may be the most intriguing of all orange varieties for their gorgeous color and their unique taste. The rind, sometimes smooth, sometimes pitted, and usually thick, may be orange with a pale pink to deep red blush, mottled, streaked, or completely scarlet, garnet, crimson, or purple-hued. Cut one open and you'll find mostly seedless flesh that can be ruby-, crimson-, or garnet-streaked or veined, or pale orange to completely blood red, scarlet, deeper purple-red, to nearly black. Blood oranges, because of their unique and often intense flavor, from very sweet to tart, and with lighter or more pronounced berry notes, are ideal for cooking, adding a unique character and fruity brightness to savory dishes, dressings and sauces, compotes, and salsa. Their striking color contrasts beautifully with sweet or navel oranges, so they are wonderful peeled and then sliced or supremed and layered in salads or desserts. The juice from more deeply hued blood oranges makes impressive glazes, ice creams and sorbets, and syrups. Like the bitter orange varieties, blood oranges have a very short season and can be found on the market through the winter, from December to March, with some varieties showing up through the spring.

Moro, Sanguinelli, and Tarocco are deeper red blood oranges with more or less intense coloration. Tarocco, an Italian variety of blood orange, medium-size with a more oval shape and paler flesh, has the reputation of being extremely sweet and flavorful and an excellent dessert orange. American varieties of Tarocco can be larger. Sanguinelli bloods have a smoother, shinier rind and are medium-size oranges that, though sweet, have little tartness or acidity. The Moro, a native of Sicily, while smaller than the other bloods with a smoother rind, is the most striking with deep purple-red, almost black flesh, sweet with a hint of raspberry.

Light, common, or half-blood orange varieties include Cara Cara or Red Navel, a navel orange whose flesh can range from pink to red; Maltaise Sanguine (as opposed to the blonde Maltaise), which are seedless and sweet with a touch of tartness; and Washington Sanguine and Doblefina, which are paler and more lightly flavored.

Orange Flavorings

ORANGE BLOSSOM WATER

Also known as orange flower water, orange blossom water is a distinctive yet delicate aromatic essence distilled from the fragrant blossoms of the bitter orange tree. Orange blossom water is a flavoring used in the cuisines of North Africa (salads, traditional sweets and desserts, and sometimes added to coffee), the Mediterranean countries (Spanish King's Cake and French madeleines), and India and Turkey. I first discovered its uses in desserts when I lived in Nantes, once a major port city welcoming ships from the French West Indies, where it is an ingredient in the city's traditional carnival donuts, *bottereaux* (beignets), and brioche-type bread, the *fouace*. Orange blossom water is very concentrated, so use it sparingly, a few drops or a teaspoon at a time. It pairs very well with carrots, berries, especially strawberries, and apricots; add it to compotes, creams and cream-based desserts, cake batters, glazes, to fish or seafood marinades. And, of course, it is deliciously intriguing with oranges. Adding a few drops of the essence to orange-based batters and creams will accentuate the orange flavor and add depth and warmth. Orange blossom water can be found in Lebanese, Indian, Middle Eastern, and gourmet food shops.

ORANGE EXTRACT

Orange extract is made from the zest of the orange and is very concentrated, so just a little should be used as an added flavoring, accentuating the orange in the dish. One-half teaspoon orange extract can be substituted for 1 tablespoon of orange zest or vice versa, whichever you have on hand. Use only 100 percent pure orange extract. Orange oil or essence is much more concentrated and thus more intense than extract, so less should be used.

LIQUEURS

Cointreau, a brand of Triple Sec, and Grand Marnier are both orange liqueurs and, the way I use them in recipes as a flavoring, are pretty interchangeable. The most striking difference is the color and mouthfeel, as Cointreau is lighter and Grand Marnier is richer, a bit heavier, and a deep amber color. Cointreau is made with a neutral sugar beet alcohol, sugar, and the peel of both Lahara bitter and sweet oranges, giving it a stronger orange nose and brighter, if lighter, taste. Grand Marnier is a blend of French cognac, sugar, and bitter Seville orange peel or essence, giving it a more caramel, faintly woodsy sweetness.

I love to add either Cointreau or Grand Marnier to a recipe when I want a splash of intense orange essence with a heady kick of spirits, but either can be replaced with orange extract or orange blossom water.

Homemade
Orange Flavorings

ORANGE POWDER

Use Orange Powder like a spice, adding a teaspoon or tablespoon to cake or muffin batter, cookie, scone, pie crust, and bread dough, and when making macaron shells. Stir into soups, stews, sauces, and marinades, dust on oatmeal or ice cream, and toss into buttered popcorn. Add it to your seasoned flour or spice rubs for meats, chicken, fish, and seafood, or spoon a bit into court bouillon. Blend orange powder with sugar or salt for baking or cooking for a wonderful citrus flavor. Orange Powder infuses most anything with a concentrated burst of orange flavor.

To make Orange Powder, preheat oven to 195 degrees F (90 degrees C). Line a large baking sheet with parchment paper.

Trim off and discard the top and bottom (stem end and blossom or navel end) of the orange, about half an inch so you can see the fruit. Slice the fruit, peel and all, as thinly as possible using either a very sharp knife or a mandolin. Spread the orange slices in a single layer on the baking sheet.

Bake until dried, about 4 hours, turning the slices over every 30 minutes for even drying. The slices are done when both the rind and the fruit center are crisp and brittle but not burned.

Remove from the oven and lift the orange slices off of the parchment and onto cooling racks. Allow to cool completely before placing in a spice blender, a coffee grinder, or a mortar and pestle and whizzing until reduced to a fine powder.

One medium orange reduces to about 5 tablespoons powder. Orange Powder will keep its fragrance and intense orange flavor for about a month if stored in the refrigerator in an airtight container.

ORANGE SUGAR

Use Orange Sugar as you would any flavored sugar or sugared topping such as cinnamon sugar: dusted on French toast, pancakes or crepes, hot buttered toast, or oatmeal. Sprinkle it rather generously on scones or muffins before baking. Sprinkle Spiced Orange Sugar over orange slices before briefly grilling in the oven. Replace granulated white sugar with Orange Sugar when whipping cream or making meringue. Stir Orange Sugar into teas or infusions and rim cocktail glasses when serving orange-based cocktails or drinks.

To make ORANGE SUGAR, finely grate the zest of 1 orange for every 1/3 cup (65 g) granulated white sugar. Increase proportionally as desired.

Put the sugar and zest in a blender or food processor and mix until the two are completely incorporated; this can also be done by rubbing the zest into the sugar with your fingertips until no lumps of zest are left. The process will not only blend the ingredients together and render them each finer, but it will cause the zest to release its intensely fragrant oils, infusing the sugar with a bright citrus flavor while tempering the bitterness of the zest. Transfer the orange sugar to a clean jar or other container with a lid. Before closing the jar, allow the sugar to dry for several hours, stirring occasionally to loosen and for even drying. Store the covered sugar at room temperature.

For CITRUS SUGAR, increase the sugar to 1/2 cup (100 g) and add the finely grated zest of 1 lemon or 1 lime with the orange zest.

For VANILLA ORANGE SUGAR, place a split vanilla bean in the jar with the Orange Sugar and allow to scent the sugar for a day or two or, ideally, longer before using. Keep the vanilla bean in the jar for as long as you have the sugar.

For MINT OR BASIL ORANGE SUGAR, add 10 to 12 fresh mint or basil leaves to the mixer with the zest and sugar before processing. Taste and add more, if desired.

For SPICED ORANGE SUGAR, add 1/4 teaspoon ground cinnamon or 1/8 teaspoon ground cardamom or nutmeg, or a bit of each, to the zest and sugar before processing. Taste and add more, if desired.

ORANGE SALT

Use Orange Salt to season raw fish and seafood in place of plain salt, or sprinkle it on baked, sautéed, grilled, or broiled fish and seafood, a simple seared chicken breast, pork or lamb chop, or steak, or to rim a margarita glass. Add it to your seasoned rub for grilling, or dust on grilled, stir-fried, or steamed vegetables. Season soups, stews, curries, risotto or pilaf, salads—especially tuna, chicken, shrimp, or egg salad—or simply replace your plain salt with orange or citrus salt in simple baked goods like muffins, scones, or breads.

To make ORANGE SALT, you will need 2 to 3 tablespoons fine orange zest for every 1/2 cup (140 g) salt, kosher salt, or flaked sea salt. Put the salt and zest in a blender or food processor and grind until the two are completely incorporated; this can also be done by rubbing the zest into the salt with your fingertips until no lumps of zest are left. Increase quantities proportionally as desired.

Spread in a single thin layer and leave in a warm, dry place or in the sun, or dry in a 200-degree F (95-degrees C) oven for 20–25 minutes, or until the orange salt is dry to the touch. Store in a lidded jar indefinitely.

For CITRUS SALT, replace 1 tablespoon of the orange zest with the zest of lime, grapefruit, or lemon—or a mix of any or all of them.

For HERBED ORANGE SALT, whiz in fresh rosemary, basil, thyme, or oregano leaves, a small pinch of chile flakes or chipotle pepper flakes, a pinch or 2 of cumin, or 1 teaspoon onion powder.

ORANGE EXTRACT

To make Orange Extract, you will need 2 to 3 large oranges for each 1 cup (250 ml) vodka. Pare the zest—without the white pith—in wide strips from the oranges with a vegetable peeler. Place the strips of zest with the vodka in a clean jar with a lid and cover tightly. Store in a cool, dark place for 1 month or longer, ideally 6–8 weeks, before straining the extract, discarding the zest, and storing the extract in the tightly lidded, sterilized jar indefinitely.

Essential Information

RECOMMENDATIONS

» Always read the recipe through completely before beginning. Components of a dish or dessert may have to be prepared in advance, chilled, marinated, or allowed to rest before cooking, baking, or assembling, sometimes for up to 24 hours; some recipes have more than one component that are best prepared in a specific order.

» Make sure that you have all of the ingredients. I urge you to weigh and measure all ingredients before beginning a recipe. I also recommend that you prepare each ingredient, chop, mince, dice, zest, juice, etc., before beginning.

» When buying oranges for cooking or baking, ideally use organic oranges whenever possible. If you cannot find organic, purchase untreated, unwaxed citrus, as you will be using the zest or the whole orange, skin and all. If using the zest or peel or the whole orange, scrub the fruit under warm running water, rinse well, and dry with a clean kitchen towel.

» Select oranges that are firm and heavy, indicating freshness and juiciness. Avoid oranges that have a soft or loose rind, feel spongy, or have any soft or discolored spots or signs of bruising; make sure there is no mold starting around the stem end. The color of the rind, whether lighter or darker orange or even orange with a green tint, is no indication of the quality or ripeness of the fruit.

» To store, always remove oranges from plastic bags or packaging, and do not wrap or cover them. Place the oranges in a bowl or platter at room temperature, in a cool but not cold place, or in the fruit or vegetable drawer of your refrigerator. Oranges will keep 1–2 weeks in or out of the refrigerator.

ORANGE SIZES AND YIELDS

» Small: 8 ounces (220 to 225 g)
» Medium-small: 9 ounces (350 g)
» Medium: 9 1/2 to 10 ounces (270 to 285 g)
» Medium-large: 11 to 12 ounces (310 to 340 g)
» Large: 13 ounces (380 g)

» 1 small juice orange will yield about 1/4 cup (65 ml) juice and a scant 1 teaspoon very fine (microplaned) packed zest, closer to 1 tablespoon loosely grated zest.

» 1 medium to large orange will yield about 1/3 to 1/2 cup (85 to 125 ml) juice, 2 small to medium oranges about 3/4 cup (185 ml) juice, and a larger orange will yield about 1/2 cup (125 ml) or more juice.

» 1 medium orange will yield about a rounded or heaping teaspoon fine zest and a large or extra-large orange will yield about a tablespoon zest.

» 1 medium orange will yield about 1 cup (250 ml, 175 g) small cubes fruit.

» Oranges will vary in size, of course, but also in sweetness, acidity or tartness, in richness of flavor, in the amount of juice, the amount of zest, and the amount of fruit it will yield depending on the variety and provenance of the orange you use as well as the time of year. Taste the orange as you may want to add a bit more or less sugar depending on the sweetness, or a squeeze of lemon or lime juice if the flavor lacks in tartness and you think it may add to the dish or dessert you are making. If I recommend a small or medium-size orange, and you can only procure extra-large ones, just use part of it.

» Where a specific quantity of orange juice or zest or fruit is best, I give the volume or weight, but where a bit more or less doesn't really change the recipe, I call for a number and size (small, medium, large) of fruit.

PREPARATION

PEEL, RIND, and SKIN are often used interchangeably. The *rind* or *skin* is the outer layer of the fruit until it is removed or peeled from the fruit, when it is referred to as the *peel*. The peel is made up of the zest and the pith; the *zest* is the colorful outer layer of the peel, which contains fragrant oils and the bright citrus flavor, while the *pith* is the spongy white inner layer, which is bitter and undesirable.

ZESTING: Using a fine microplane zester will give you the finest possible zest, releasing a more intense burst of the flavorful oils with less bitterness once incorporated into a dish. Some zesters specifically designed for citrus have a snap-on attachment behind the grating holes that catches all of the zest, which is ideal. If you do not have a microplane zester, using a cheese grater is fine, but the zest may be coarser; you can mince it finer with a knife. Draw the zester back and forth against the orange, moving around the orange, scratching only the colored zest and avoiding the white pith. Zest can be added to almost anything, from sauces, creams, dressings, and syrups, to dough and batter, or even pushed under the skin of poultry and rubbed into meat. The uses, as you will see from the recipes, are endless.

» If a recipe calls only for the zest or peel of an orange, press the juice from the orange first to use for another recipe or measure and freeze in a ziplock or sealable plastic bag, marking the amount on the bag.

» You can also use the zest to make Orange Sugar (page 21) or Orange Salt (page 22), or peel off the zest in strips to make your own Orange Extract (page 18), or add to sauces, stews, or tea to infuse with flavor. Or simply spread the zest, grated or in strips, on a parchment-lined baking sheet and allow to dry at room temperature or out in the sun for 24–48 hours until dry and curled. Bake at your oven's lowest temperature until super dry and crispy then finely grind and save in an airtight container to use in place of fresh zest or extract. Or dry the strips, store in an airtight container, and use to infuse tea. And if you find yourself with a windfall of oranges, too many to eat or use in a short amount of time, use a few to make Orange Powder (page 19).

PARING: Paring an orange is when you remove a long, wide strip of the zest from the peel using a vegetable peeler or sharp paring knife without the white pith underneath. Simply press the vegetable peeler or paring knife into the zest and, applying a bit of pressure, pull down slowly to remove a 2- to 3-inch (5 to 7 1/2 cm) long strip about 1 inch (2 1/2 cm) wide. These wide strips of zest are used to flavor savory or sweet sauces, syrups, and creams, as well as stews during cooking or simmering; the strip of peel or zest is then removed and discarded before serving. Add a strip of zest to your teapot when steeping tea for a hint of citrus. Use it in cocktails or for making orange extract. Strips of zest pared from the orange can be finely diced or minced with a knife if you have no zester.

» Halfway between using a microplane zester and a vegetable peeler is using a citrus zester. A citrus zester is a tool with a row of 5 tiny holes that, when dragged across the surface of the orange, removes the zest in long, thin curls. These can be tossed in sauces or soups, candied lightly in syrup to use as pretty decoration on cakes, garnish for salads, main dishes, or cocktails.

PEELING: Peeling an orange can also mean removing the entire rind including the white pith using a sharp knife to expose the flesh of the orange in its entirety. Using a very sharp knife longer than the orange is wide—do not use a short-bladed paring knife—cut off both ends of the rind (stem and navel or blossom ends) to reveal a full circle of fruit. Place the orange flat on your cutting board on one of the cut ends. Place the blade of the knife on the line where the white pith meets the flesh and cut down following the curve of the orange. Continue cutting around the orange, following the line where pith meets fruit, removing strips of rind, all the white pith, and the outer membrane of the orange while trying to cut off as little fruit flesh as possible. Once done, trim off any white pith still attached to the fruit.

SLICING: Once the rind and all pith are removed from the fruit, cut slices horizontally across the core, popping out the spongy white center core and discarding, leaving you with rounds of pure orange fruit.

SEGMENTING: A segment is a wedge of orange still in its membrane. Simply peel the orange with your fingers and pull apart the segments. A supreme (see below) can also be referred to as a segment. Segments can be added to salads, cut into cubes or chunks to top cakes and breads, or eaten as is.

SUPREMING: A supreme of a citrus fruit is a wedge or section of the fruit without the membrane that separates the sections. Hold the peeled fruit in one hand—over a bowl to catch runoff juices—and a sharp knife in the other. Carefully cut out the segments of orange, slicing down as close to the membrane as possible, angling the knife towards the center. Repeat on the other side of the segment or wedge, cutting the fruit away from the other membrane and the core. Continue with the remaining sections. Squeeze the juice out from the membranes/core left in your hand. Supremes are wonderful in salads, desserts, cakes, soups, etc.

JUICING: This is a simple one. Juicing an orange is squeezing out every last drop of the juice while catching and separating out the seeds and pulp. A multitude of tools are available for juicing your favorite citrus fruit—one for every budget, need, or desire, the amount of storage, countertop, or drawer space you have, and, of course, depending on how often you'll be juicing oranges. There is a two-handled, hinged, or handheld squeezer; an electric juicer; a bowl with fitted juicer/strainer (manual); a motorized or manual orange press; or a handheld wooden reamer. But whether electric, motorized, manual, stand, tabletop, handheld, or one that simply sits atop a bowl, whether costly or inexpensive, choose the one that works the best and that is the most comfortable for you. The goal is to squeeze out the juice of an orange, and every one does the job.

» If using only the juice or the flesh of the fruit, zest the orange first and save in the freezer in a sealed plastic bag for up to three months or in the refrigerator for up to a week.

MEASURING and EQUIVALENTS

I've included metric measures (ml and g) after the US Standard measurements (dry and liquid cups). Teaspoons and tablespoons are pretty universal, so I only specified weights if I thought that it made a difference (cocoa powder, for example). Some measurement conversions have been rounded up or rounded down for easier measuring.

The better the quality of the ingredients you use, the better tasting the finished dish or baked goods will be. But don't let that disconcert you or send you scrambling for more expensive brands. My recipe testers live all over the country (and the world), some are chefs but most are home cooks, and in testing the recipes in *Orange Appeal,* used the ingredients that they had on hand, in their pantries, or what was available in their local supermarkets, so no two used the same brands or bought at the same stores. And the recipes worked for each of them. Just be aware that some staple ingredients do differ from country to country, from brand to brand, so slight adjustments may have to be made. Some brands of butter, for example, have higher fat or water content; brands of flour differ; etc. The size of oranges, onions, fennel bulbs, etc., may vary, so use your instincts and adjust the recipe or the ingredient accordingly.

FLOUR: Where the type of flour isn't specified, use all-purpose. My method for measuring flour is simple and consistent: using a tablespoon, stir the flour to lighten, scoop, and place in the measuring cup. Do not pack or tamp it down, do not tap the cup on the work surface as the quantity of flour will change. Once you have spooned flour into the measuring cup to overflowing, level the flour with a flat utensil such as the straight back of a knife blade.

» 1 cup of flour weighs 4.8 ounces / 135 g

SUGAR: Where the type of sugar isn't specified, use granulated white sugar.

» 1 cup granulated white sugar equals 7 ounces / 200 g
» 1 cup packed brown sugar, light or dark equals 7 ounces / 200 g

BUTTER: Most of my recipes use unsalted butter, although a couple of the French recipes use salted butter, and I have specified this in the ingredients. Feel free to use salted butter, but adjust the salt in the recipe if you believe that it will affect the taste of the dish or dessert.

» 1 tablespoon butter equals 1/2 ounce / 15 g

EGGS: I use large eggs for all of my baking and cooking.

» 1 large caliber French egg weighs approximately 2.1 to 2.3 ounces / 60 to 65 g

OUNCES TO GRAMS: 1 ounce equals 28.34 g (g equal amount in ounces x 28.34); I round up to 30 g.

» Pinch equals 1/16 teaspoon equals 0.3 ml

» Large pinch equals 1/8 teaspoon equals 0.6 ml

» 1 pound equals 16 ounces equals 450 g

LIQUID MEASURES

I TEASPOON	5 ML		
I TABLESPOON	3 TEASPOONS	1/16 CUP	15 ML
1/8 CUP	2 TABLESPOONS	I FLUID OUNCES	
1/4 CUP	4.5 TABLESPOONS	2 FLUID OUNCES	60 ML
1/3 CUP	6 TABLESPOONS	2.6 FLUID OUNCES	80 ML
1/2 CUP	9 TABLESPOONS	4 FLUID OUNCES	125 ML
3/4 CUP	13.5 TABLESPOONS	6 FLUID OUNCES	185 ML
I CUP	18 TABLESPOONS	8 FLUID OUNCES	250 ML
2 CUPS	I PINT		500 ML
4 CUPS	I QUART		I LITER

» 1 American standard cup equals 8 fluid ounces / British standard cup equals 10 fluid ounces

DRY MEASURES (WEIGHT VARIES DEPENDING ON THE INGREDIENT)

I TABLESPOON	3 TEASPOONS	1/16 CUP
2 TABLESPOONS	1/8 CUP	
5 1/3 TABLESPOONS	1/3 CUP	
8 TABLESPOONS	1/2 CUP	
12 TABLESPOONS	3/4 CUP	
16 TABLESPOONS	I CUP	

OVEN TEMPERATURES

195 DEGREES F	90 DEGREES C
225 DEGREES F	110 DEGREES C
250 DEGREES F	130 DEGREES C
275 DEGREES F	140 DEGREES C
300 DEGREES F	150 DEGREES C
325 DEGREES F	170 DEGREES C
350 DEGREES F	180 DEGREES C
375 DEGREES F	190 DEGREES C
400 DEGREES F	200 DEGREES C
425 DEGREES F	220 DEGREES C

Sauces,
Dressings,
Dips,
and Relishes

Orange-Fig Sauce

Makes 1 cup (250 ml)

1 tablespoon Dijon-style mustard

1 small or medium orange, finely zested

1/8 teaspoon Orange Salt (page 22), table, or sea salt

2/3 to 3/4 cup (150 to 175 ml) freshly squeezed orange juice, about 2 oranges

Freshly ground black pepper, to taste

1/2 cup (125 ml / 5.7 ounces / 165 g) good-quality fig or fig-orange jam

THIS WARM, SAVORY SAUCE IS A PLAY ON THE TRADITIONAL orange-currant sauce, but instead brings together the perfect pairing of oranges and figs. Orange-Fig Sauce is a snap to put together and takes only a few minutes on the stove to heat and thicken. Serve this intriguing sauce with roast duck or chicken, lamb, veal, or ham, roasts or chops, or brush onto meats while grilling. This would be equally delicious using red currant or plum jam in place of the fig jam.

Whisk the mustard, zest, and salt into the orange juice until the mustard has dissolved. Add a few grindings of black pepper. Whisk in the jam until dissolved.

Place the ingredients in a small saucepan over medium-low heat and bring to a simmer. Cook, whisking for 8–10 minutes, keeping the sauce at a simmer until slightly reduced and thickened. Serve warm.

(see page 36 for Sweet and Spicy Caramelized Onion, Raisin, and Orange Compote.)

Sweet-and-Spicy Caramelized Onion, Raisin, and Orange Compote

Makes 2 cups (500 ml)

2 medium yellow onions

1 tablespoon olive oil

1 tablespoon butter or margarine
  (1/2 ounce /15 g)

1/2 cup (70 g) raisins or sultanas

3/4 to 1 teaspoon ras el hanout,
  for more or less heat

1/4 teaspoon ground cinnamon

3/4 to 1 teaspoon orange zest

Salt and freshly ground black
  pepper, to taste

1/4 cup (65 ml) orange juice

1/4 teaspoon cornstarch

1/2 cup (125 ml) water

1 cup (250 ml, 175 g) small
  orange cubes

SERVE THIS SPICY, SAVORY, AND SWEET COMPOTE as a condiment for hot or cold roasted or grilled meats or chicken, or a cheese platter. Create an appetizer crostini by topping thin rounds of gingerbread or toasted baguette, or splitting and filling 2-inch (5 cm) Sweet Potato Biscuits (page 113) with fresh or demi-sec goat cheese, bleu cheese, or aged cheddar, and a teaspoon of the compote.

Peel and trim the onions and halve. Slice the onions rather thickly, about 1/4 inch (1/2 cm) wide, and separate into strips. Heat the oil and butter in a large skillet or sauté pan over medium-low heat until sizzling; add the onions and toss to coat with the fat. Lower the heat slightly and cook the onions slowly, stirring, until the onions are very soft and tender, transparent, and caramelized to a golden brown, 12–14 minutes.

Add the raisins, ras el hanout, cinnamon, orange zest, a pinch each of salt and pepper, and the orange juice. Stir and let the onions cook just until the juice has reduced and thickened, 1–2 minutes.

Dissolve the cornstarch in the water and add to the pan. Adjust the heat so the liquid is at a low simmer, and allow the onions to cook, stirring, for 7–9 minutes until the liquid reduces almost completely, the raisins are plump, and the onions become meltingly tender without dissolving. Stir in the orange chunks and cook until heated through. Store in the refrigerator for up to a week.

(see page 35 for photo)

Blood Orange Salsa
with Avocado or Beet

Makes scant 2 cups (450 ml)
or more

2 medium to large blood oranges

1/2 to 3/4 red onion, diced

3 tablespoons finely chopped fresh cilantro (coriander)

1 chipotle chile pepper in adobo sauce, pepper only

2 tablespoons olive oil

2 tablespoons lime juice

Pinch of salt

Pinch of freshly ground black pepper

1 ripe avocado or 1 small roasted beet

SALSA IS ONE OF THOSE CONDIMENTS that can easily be changed or adjusted to taste and easily increased in quantity, to serve a family or a crowd. You can make the salsa as mild or as hot as you like by adding more or less chipotle pepper, or replace the chipotle pepper with 1/2 or more diced jalapeño or a milder fresh pepper. Add more avocado or beet or even a garden-fresh tomato or two during the summer months to add more body and flavor complexity to the salsa.

Make the salsa early in the day, allowing an hour or more for the flavors to meld, although letting it rest in the refrigerator overnight is even better. Serve with tortilla or pita chips as a dip, or serve as a condiment to seared or grilled fish, scallops, or shrimp, over breaded veal chops or fish filets, on tacos or burgers, or pile it onto a salad.

Prepare the salsa by first removing the peel, white pith, and white spongy core of the oranges. Cut the fruit into bite-size chunks or dice and place in a medium bowl. Add the onion and cilantro.

Slice the chipotle pepper and scrape out and discard the seeds; finely chop the pepper and add to the salsa. Add the oil, lime juice, salt, and pepper; toss to blend. Peel the avocado or the beet, cut into small cubes, and fold into the salsa.

Taste the salsa, adding more chipotle pepper, if you like your salsa hot, and salt and pepper as desired. Cover and place in the refrigerator for at least 30 minutes for the flavors to meld before enjoying.

Three Tasty Orange Salad Dressings

1/2 cup (125 ml) full-fat buttermilk

2 tablespoons crème fraîche

2 tablespoons olive oil

1/4 cup (65 ml) orange juice

2 teaspoons lime juice

1 small orange, finely zested

1 small lime, finely zested

1 teaspoon honey or balsamic reduction

1/2 teaspoon minced fresh or 1/4 teaspoon dried rosemary

1/2 teaspoon minced fresh or 1/4 teaspoon dried thyme

1/2 teaspoon minced fresh or 1/4 teaspoon dried basil

Salt and freshly ground black pepper, to taste

Creamy Herbed Buttermilk Citrus Dressing

Makes 1 cup (250 ml)

TRY THIS BRIGHT, FLAVORFUL BUTTERMILK DRESSING on a salad of shredded kale, sucrine, or romaine, purple cabbage or radicchio, or tossed with orange supremes, avocado, and apple or pear chunks. Top with lightly toasted pine nuts and crumbled bleu cheese. Or try on a savory-sweet salad of sliced celery, cucumbers, carrots, and red bell peppers with apple or pear wedges, a handful of raisins or dried berries, and topped with mixed seeds. Use whatever fresh herbs you have in your garden. Crème fraîche is the best consistency and mild tartness for this recipe, but feel free to use sour cream or even mascarpone in its place to add flavor and body.

Whisk all of the ingredients together. Chill until ready to serve, whisking well before serving.

(continued)

1/4 cup (65 ml) orange juice

2 sprigs fresh rosemary, leaves only, finely chopped

1 to 2 sprigs fresh thyme or lemon thyme, leaves and flowers only, chopped

2 tablespoons white wine or champagne vinegar

Salt and freshly ground black pepper, to taste

1/4 to 1/2 cup (65 to 125 ml) olive oil

Rosemary Orange Vinaigrette

Makes 1/2 to 3/4 cup (125 to 185 ml)

PERFECT OVER A SALAD OF THINLY SLICED PEARS, Medjool dates, and red onion on a bed of Cara Cara, navelina, or blood oranges. Or try it on a grilled romaine, radicchio, or sucrine and chicken salad with sweet heirloom or cherry tomatoes, bitter arugula, and salty feta or bleu cheese.

Whisk together all of the ingredients except the oil. Continue whisking as you gradually pour 1/4 cup of oil into the vinaigrette; whisk in up to 1/4 cup more oil as desired. Taste and add more seasoning as desired.

---

1 tablespoon Dijon-style mustard

2 tablespoons red wine or raspberry vinegar

Freshly ground black pepper, to taste

1/4 cup (65 ml) freshly squeezed orange juice

1/4 to 1/2 cup (65 to 125 ml) good-quality mild extra virgin olive oil

Orange Mustard Vinaigrette

Makes about 3/4 cup (185 ml)

THIS IS IDEAL TOSSED INTO MIXED GREENS or lamb's lettuce and cubes of roasted beets then topped with orange slices and goat cheese or feta. It is also wonderful when tossed into a salad of mixed greens, roasted and shredded chicken, shaved Brussels sprouts, grapes, and chunks of orange.

Whisk the mustard, vinegar, and a generous grinding of pepper together until blended and smooth. Whisk in the orange juice and then 1/4 cup of oil in a slow, steady stream until emulsified; add up to 1/4 cup more oil as desired.

Blood Orange
Hummus Vinaigrette

Makes a scant 2/3 cup
(150 ml)

2 tablespoons vegetable or
  olive oil

2 tablespoons sesame oil

1 tablespoon white wine or
  champagne vinegar

2 tablespoons blood orange juice

1 small blood orange, zested,
  optional

3 tablespoons hummus

Freshly ground black pepper, to
  taste

THE ADDITION OF HUMMUS, a thick Middle Eastern dip of puréed chickpeas, tahini sesame seed paste, olive oil, lemon juice, salt, and garlic, to this delicious vinaigrette not only adds body and creaminess, but adds a nuttiness that pairs wonderfully with orange. I'm absolutely crazy about this dressing and toss it into salads, drizzle it on grilled fresh radicchio, treviso, romaine hearts, or sucrine and orange wedges, serve it with grilled shrimp, or use it for chicken salad. Use homemade or any good-quality store-bought hummus.

Measure all of the ingredients into a small bowl and whisk until well blended and smooth.

Orange Avocado Salad Dressing or Dip

Makes 1 cup (250 ml)

1 teaspoon Dijon-style mustard

2 teaspoons white wine vinegar

Salt and freshly ground black pepper, to taste

1 large egg yolk

3/8 cup (100 ml) olive oil

1 ripe avocado

6 tablespoons orange juice

1 tablespoon lime juice

Pinch of chipotle chile powder or a few drops of hot sauce, to taste

2 to 3 tablespoons chopped fresh cilantro (coriander)

A SIMPLE BLEND OF HOMEMADE MAYONNAISE (so much easier than you think) tangy with white wine vinegar and heady with mustard, mashed avocados, and orange juice. Add to this a squeeze of lime and fragrant fresh cilantro, and you have a flavorful yet delicate and well-balanced blend that can be used either as a salad dressing or as a dip with raw vegetables, steamed shrimp, or tortilla chips.

Whisk the mustard, vinegar, and a little salt and pepper into the egg yolk. Using a fork, or a whisk, blend the oil into the yolk, pouring the oil into the bowl in a slow, steady stream as you whisk. The mixture should emulsify into a thick and creamy mayonnaise.

Scoop the avocado out of the peel, discarding peel and pit, and mash with a fork until smooth. Whisk the avocado mash into the mayonnaise. Whisk in the orange and lime juices, and then the chile powder and cilantro. Taste and add more salt, pepper, chile powder, or cilantro as desired. You can also add more orange or lime juice if you like.

Sweet-and-Sour Beurre Blanc or Rouge

Makes ²/₃ cup (150 ml)

1 medium Cara Cara or other sweet juice orange

1 small to medium blood orange

1 tablespoon balsamic vinegar concentrate or reduction, either dark or white

1 teaspoon olive oil

1 purple shallot, chopped

Salt and freshly ground black pepper, to taste

1 1/2 tablespoons (3/4 ounce / 22 g) unsalted butter, cut into about 6 small cubes

A *BEURRE BLANC* IS A CLASSIC FRENCH SAUCE traditionally served over fish. Delicate yet flavorful, beurre blanc is a white wine reduction with shallots into which butter (*beurre*) is whisked into the syrupy reduction to give it a rich, smooth consistency. I was always terrified of making this, thinking it fussy and complicated and time consuming, until our friend Stéphane whipped one up in our kitchen to serve over a fish and seafood *choucroute*. I discovered that with only a few ingredients and 6–7 minutes, you can create an impressive and flavorful sauce. This isn't a true beurre blanc because there is no wine in it, but it is based on the same simple technique, and the resulting sauce will be either *blanc*, light, or *rouge*, red, depending on the balsamic reduction you use. Savory, acidic, and sweet, this is a fantastic sauce to drizzle over lamb chops, fish, asparagus, or other steamed, roasted, or grilled vegetables.

Finely zest the Cara Cara and then squeeze both oranges for a total of 1/2 cup (125 ml) juice. Place the zest with the juice, balsamic concentrate, and oil in a small to medium heavy-bottom saucepan. Add the shallot to the saucepan, season with salt and pepper, and bring to a boil over medium heat.

Lower the heat slightly and allow the liquid to boil for 5 minutes, whisking constantly, until reduced and syrupy. Whisk in the cubes of butter, one at a time, allowing each to melt before adding and whisking in the next cube. Serve hot.

Spiced Cranberry Orange Relish

Makes 3 cups (750 ml)

1 1/2 cups (375 ml) water, divided

3 cups (12 ounces / 340 g) fresh cranberries

1 medium-large juice orange

1/4 cup (65 ml) honey

1 teaspoon ground ginger

1/8 teaspoon ground cinnamon

1/8 teaspoon ground cloves

1/8 teaspoon ground cardamom

CRANBERRY RELISH IS TRULY A CLASSIC AMERICAN condiment and is unfailingly found on all Thanksgiving and Christmas tables. Or it should be. This spiced orangey relish is my brother Michael's version: spicy, tart, and sweet, the perfect accompaniment to roasted chicken, turkey, or any other kind of poultry. It would be equally tasty with roasted and grilled meat or piled onto a sandwich. Chilling the relish before serving allows the flavors to blend and balance the bitterness of the cranberries, mellowing into sweetness. For more orange flavor, replace the 1/2 cup (125 ml) water added with the orange chunks with orange juice.

Heat 1 cup (250 ml) of water in a medium saucepan. Add the cranberries and bring to a boil. Lower heat and simmer, covered, for 10 minutes. Remove lid and simmer uncovered for 10 minutes more.

Finely zest the orange and reserve. Peel the orange, discarding the rind and white pith, and cut the fruit into chunks, catching all of the runoff juice that you can.

Add the orange chunks and juice, orange zest, remaining 1/2 cup (125 ml) water, honey, ginger, cinnamon, cloves, and cardamom to the cooked cranberries. Continue simmering on low heat, stirring often, for 20 minutes.

Remove from heat and allow to cool to room temperature. Transfer to a bowl and refrigerate before serving.

White Bean and Artichoke Hummus

2 medium oranges

1 can (14 or 15 ounces / 400 or 425 g) white beans, drained and rinsed (about 1 3/4 cups / 300 g)

1 jar (12 1/2 ounces / 360 g) marinated artichoke hearts, drained, divided

3 1/2 ounces (100 g) feta cheese, divided

2 tablespoons crème fraîche, natural Greek yogurt, or sour cream

2 tablespoons sesame oil

1 teaspoon lime juice, or more to taste

Salt and freshly ground black pepper, to taste

4 tablespoons chopped fresh cilantro (coriander) or basil leaves

THIS DELICATE BUT PERFUMED DIP is as healthy as it is addictive, and it makes a great hummus-type dip for chips or crudités (raw vegetables). It is quick to put together as it uses canned beans and jarred marinated artichoke hearts, and the flavors can be adjusted to taste by simply folding more chopped feta, artichoke hearts, or cubes of orange into the hummus, or adding a bit of chopped garlic if you like. I love this spooned onto a salad or spread on toasted slices of baguette or pain de campagne and topped with Orange, Tomato, and Red Onion Salsa (page 88) for a fresh, healthful, vegetarian lunch bruschetta. It keeps in the refrigerator for up to a week, the flavors developing when chilled.

Finely zest and juice 1 of the oranges; peel the second orange and cut into small cubes, setting aside.

Place the beans, 2/3 of the artichoke hearts, 1/2 of the feta cheese, the crème fraîche, sesame oil, lime juice, orange zest, a scant 1/3 cup (75 ml) of the orange juice, and salt and pepper in a food processor, and purée until smooth. Scrape into a large bowl. If the dip is too thick, whisk in as much of the remaining orange juice as needed for desired consistency. Crumble the rest of the feta cheese and thinly slice or coarsely chop the remaining artichoke hearts then fold both into the hummus with the chopped fresh cilantro and the orange cubes. Taste, adding more salt and pepper if needed.

Indian Sweet-and-Sour Tamarind Citrus Peel Condiment

Makes scant 1 cup (225 ml)

2 Mandarin oranges

2 small to medium oranges (juice, blood, or navel)

4 teaspoons vegetable oil

TEMPERING INGREDIENTS

1 teaspoon black mustard seeds

2 dried red chiles, halved

4 teaspoons sesame seeds, divided

1/4 teaspoon ground turmeric

1/8 teaspoon asafoetida

SPICE MIX

3/8 teaspoon chili powder

1/2 teaspoon ground cumin

5/8 teaspoon ground coriander

1/4 teaspoon fenugreek seeds

6 black peppercorns

1/2 teaspoon salt, plus more to taste

1 tablespoon tamarind paste

1 1/2 cups (375 ml) warm water

3 teaspoons light brown sugar

GARNISH

8 to 10 curry leaves

1 teaspoon vegetable oil

GOJJU IS A SWEET-AND-SOUR CONDIMENT, sauce, or side dish from India traditionally made with a mix of bitter or sour ingredients with sweet, such as bitter gourd, pineapple, and tomato. This is my friend Deepa Gopinath's version from the Malda district in Karnataka, a recipe she learned from her mother, Geetha, as a way to use up Mandarin and orange peels that would otherwise be discarded. Don't be put off by the daunting list of ingredients; it is well worth the effort!

The sauce is puckery sour and sweet with a nice backdrop of heat from the chile pepper, while the orange and Mandarin peels add a beautiful bitter endnote to the sweet. This warm, complex gojju can be stirred through rice or served as a dip with your favorite flatbread, chapati, samosas, or pakora.

It's important to have all of the ingredients measured and ready before starting to toast the spices and make the gojju. Feel free to substitute up to 1/2 cup (125 ml) Mandarin or orange juice for part of the water.

Peel the Mandarins. Eat the fruit or use for another purpose, reserving only the rinds. Using a sharp peeler, remove the zest only from the 2 oranges, being careful to avoid the white pith. Finely dice both the Mandarin peel and the orange zest, keeping each separate.

In a large skillet, heat the oil over medium heat until the surface is shimmering but not yet smoking. Turn the heat down to low and add the mustard seeds. When most of the seeds have popped, add the chiles, 1/2 teaspoon sesame seeds, turmeric, and asafoetida. Continue to cook over low heat, stirring, until the sesame seeds are golden.

Add the diced Mandarin peel to the skillet and cook on low heat for 5–7 minutes, stirring occasionally. Add the orange zest and continue to cook for another 10 minutes until the peel is crisp.

While waiting for the peel to crisp, dry roast the remaining sesame seeds in a small heavy-bottom pan, stirring continuously. When the seeds are golden brown, remove from heat. Allow to cool, and then grind to a powder with a spice grinder or mortar and pestle; set aside.

Wipe out the pan and add the chili powder, cumin, coriander, fenugreek seeds, and peppercorns. Dry roast together on low heat, stirring continuously. When the spices are fragrant, remove from heat and allow to cool, and then grind to a powder.

Add the powdered spice mix and salt to the pan with the now crisped peel. Fry on low heat for 1–2 minutes, stirring constantly. Add the tamarind paste and warm water. Stir in the ground sesame seeds and simmer for 5–6 minutes over medium heat, stirring occasionally. Add the brown sugar, stir, and cook until dissolved. Taste, and add a little more salt if needed.

The mixture should be a thick sauce consistency, although it will continue to thicken a bit once off the heat. If it is too thin, keep on the heat, stirring, until it thickens. If it is too thick, add just enough water, a teaspoon at a time, until thinned to a thick sauce.

Just before serving, prepare the curry leaves. Heat the oil in the pan used to heat the spices, adding the curry leaves to the hot oil and cooking until the leaves are crisped. Add the crisped leaves to the sauce as a garnish.

Soups, Salads, Starters, and Sides

Spiced Red Lentil and Carrot Soup

Serves 4

1 cup (6 ounces / 170 g) red or coral lentils

2 tablespoons olive oil

3 sweet carrots (8 ounces / 225 g) peeled and chopped

1 medium onion, peeled and chopped

2 cloves garlic, peeled and minced

1 orange, finely zested

3 1/2 cups (875 ml) light vegetable stock or water

1 cup (250 ml) orange juice

1 teaspoon ground turmeric

1 teaspoon ground cumin

1/4 teaspoon ground cardamom

1/4 teaspoon ground ginger

2 teaspoons dried coriander leaves or 1 teaspoon ground coriander

1/2 teaspoon salt, or more to taste

1 dried ñora pepper, split in half up to the stem, white seeds removed, optional

Greek yogurt, for garnish

Chopped fresh cilantro (coriander), for garnish

HEALTHFUL AND WARMING, this Spiced Red Lentil and Carrot Soup is kissed with the sweetness of orange and deliciously infused with spices reminiscent of Indian cuisine. A swirl of yogurt and a dusting of fresh cilantro give this comforting soup a bright, cool, tangy touch. Cook it down a bit until thick, and serve it like an Indian lentil dal over rice or pilaf as a different serving option.

Rinse the lentils under cool running water, drain, and set aside.

Heat the olive oil in a soup pot and sauté the carrots, onions, garlic, and zest until the carrots and onion soften and the onion is translucent, about 5 minutes. Add the lentils, the water, orange juice, spices, coriander, salt, and the dried ñora pepper, if using, to the pot. Bring to a boil, lower the heat, and simmer until the lentils are cooked and the carrots are tender, 20–25 minutes.

Remove the pot from the heat, remove and discard the ñora pepper, and purée the soup either in a blender or with an immersion blender, adding a bit more water if you like a thinner soup.

Heat the soup gently before serving if made ahead of time. To serve, ladle the soup into 4 bowls, swirl 1 to 2 tablespoons of Greek yogurt in each bowl, and top with fresh cilantro.

Chilled White Asparagus Velouté with Orange Chantilly

Serves 6

25 ounces (700 g) fresh white asparagus

4 cups (1 l) water

1/2 teaspoon salt

3 tablespoons (1 1/2 ounces / 45 g) butter

3 tablespoons (30 g) all-purpose flour

1/2 cup (125 ml) dry white wine

Salt and freshly ground black pepper, to taste

1/8 teaspoon ground cumin, plus more to taste

1 large egg yolk

1 cup (250 ml) heavy cream, chilled and divided

1/2 cup plus 3 tablespoons (170 ml) freshly squeezed orange juice, divided

1/2 teaspoon finely grated orange zest

Olive oil, for serving

ASPARAGUS AND ORANGE ARE A WONDERFUL AND POPULAR combination, from asparagus salads or mousse, to steamed asparagus topped with an orange cream or sauce. So why not soup? Technically, this soup is a *velouté*, a smooth, often delicately flavored, cream soup thickened with a roux, butter, egg yolks, and cream. But chilled, this wonderful soup takes on the personality of a gazpacho, very light and refreshing, making a sophisticated summer starter or as part of a light lunch.

While *velouté d'asperges* is commonly made with tender green asparagus when paired with orange, I chose to use white asparagus for its more delicate, less "grassy" flavor, allowing the sweet orange flavor to come through. Plump white asparagus, sometimes turning towards violet, are a specialty of the Loire area of France where I have lived for more than a dozen years. I think it is particularly better suited to pairing with orange, both flavors evident in every mouthful. The pale creamy color and the delicate savor make a very elegant soup.

White asparagus needs special treatment, as the outer layer of the spear can be tough and stringy or woody. Peel the bottom two-thirds of each asparagus spear, or you will find sharp strings of it in your otherwise smooth soup.

Wash the asparagus; snap or slice off the hard base of each spear, about 1 to 1 1/2 inches (2 to 4 cm), and discard. Slice off the tip of each spear, about 2 inches (5 cm) from the top, to be used for garnish. Using a vegetable peeler or a paring knife, peel the tough, woody outer layer off of each spear and slice the spears into 1-inch (2 cm) chunks.

Place the asparagus tips and chunks in a pot with the water and 1/2 teaspoon of salt. Bring to a boil over medium heat, and then lower and simmer gently until the asparagus tips are fork tender, 10–15 minutes. Carefully remove 12 tips and set aside; allow the remaining asparagus to continue to simmer for another 10 minutes, or until very soft. Place a colander over a heat-resistant bowl and drain the asparagus, reserving the liquid for the soup.

In the same pot over low heat, melt the butter and add the flour all at once. Whisking continuously and vigorously, cook the roux until completely smooth and thickened, about 1 minute. Whisk in the wine and cook until the alcohol evaporates, not more than 2 minutes. Slowly add back the asparagus cooking liquid, 1 ladle at a time, whisking after each addition until thickened and smooth.

Once all the cooking liquid has been returned to the pot and the soup is smooth and slightly thickened, add the cooked asparagus from the colander (not the reserved tips) and purée the soup with an immersion blender or in a stand blender until perfectly smooth. Add the reserved tips back into the soup; season with salt and pepper. Stir in the cumin. Allow the soup to simmer gently for 2 minutes.

Whisk the egg yolk together with $1/2$ cup (125 ml) of cream in a small bowl until blended and smooth; whisk in $1/2$ cup (125 ml) orange juice. Whisk 1 ladle of the hot soup into the egg mixture, then a second, and continue whisking about half of the hot soup into the bowl, 1 ladle at a time; this will gently and gradually heat the egg mixture. Add this back to the pot. Remove the soup from the heat and allow to cool to room temperature. Place the soup, covered, in the refrigerator to chill overnight.

Just before serving, whip the remaining cream until thick and holding fairly firm peaks. Beat in the orange zest, and then the remaining orange juice, 1 tablespoon at a time. Place 2 asparagus tips from the 12 tips you set aside in each of 6 small bowls then ladle soup into each bowl. Drizzle about 1 tablespoon of oil in a swirl atop the soup in each bowl, add a dollop of the orange whipped cream, and serve immediately.

Orange, Red Onion, Fennel, and Carrot Salad

Serves 4 as a starter or side dish, or serves 2 to 3 as a light lunch

DRESSING

3 tablespoons olive oil

3 tablespoons white wine vinegar or cider vinegar

2 teaspoons honey

1 orange, zested

1 to 2 dried chile peppers of choice, toasted and crushed, or 1/4 to 1/2 teaspoon chipotle chili powder, or 1/2 teaspoon ground coriander

Salt and freshly ground black pepper, to taste

Juice from the salad oranges

SALAD

2 large navel, juice, or blood oranges

1 fennel bulb

1 sweet carrot

1/2 small or medium red onion, peeled

Fennel fronds, chopped

Mint leaves or fresh chives, finely chopped, optional

SWEET, FRUITY ORANGE HAS A NATURAL AFFINITY for both fennel, with its slightly licorice flavor, and tangy red onions. The addition of a carrot to this refreshing salad adds a bit more sweetness to complement the kick of the onion and fennel while increasing the satisfying crunch. The sweetness of the vinaigrette is balanced with the smoky heat of the chili powder, adding more complexity and depth to the flavors of a truly simple salad. The feathery fronds sticking out willy-nilly from the branches on top of the fennel bulb are a delicious addition to a salad when used like any fresh herb, finely chopped and sprinkled over the top.

Dressing

Whisk together thoroughly the oil, vinegar, honey, zest, crushed chiles or chili powder, and salt and pepper. Set aside.

Salad

Peel both oranges, making sure to remove all of the white pith. Slice the oranges thinly in rounds, collecting the juice that runs off. Place the orange slices in a wide serving dish or bowl. Whisk the juice from the oranges into the salad dressing.

Trim the fennel bulb, cutting off and discarding the stem-like branches on top, the thick, tough bottom, and any thick, tough outer layers, reserving the feathery fronds. Slice the bulb as thinly as possible and then julienne the slices. Layer the fennel over the top of the orange rounds.

(continued)

Trim and peel the carrot, cut in half or thirds, and then julienne into thin matchsticks or slice into thin coins. Layer the carrots over the fennel. Cut the onion into very thin slices, separating into strips, and add to the salad.

Spoon about 3/4 of the dressing all over the salad, cover with plastic wrap, and refrigerate until serving time. When ready to serve, dust the salad with the chopped fennel fronds and mint or chives. Serve with remaining dressing on the side.

NOTE: The amount of chili powder you add to your dressing depends greatly on the kind of chili powder or roasted chiles you use, whether they are hotter or smokier, as well as how much of a bite you want to add to your salad. Start with a small amount and taste before adding more. I use chipotle chili powder and love the flavor, so I tend to be rather heavy-handed, knowing that it adds a smokier flavor rather than a spicier one. My friend, Elizabeth Morris, who generously shared her version of the recipe with me, toasted dried cayenne chiles in a skillet and crushed them. For a spicy warmth without the heat, replace the crushed chile with 1/2 teaspoon of ground coriander.

Pea and Shiitake Orange Risotto

Serves 6 as a side dish
or starter, serves 4 as a
main dish

2 tablespoons butter or
  margarine, divided

2 tablespoons olive oil, divided,
  plus more as needed

8.8 ounces (250 g) shiitake
  mushrooms, stems removed,
  caps sliced into 1/4- to 1/2-inch
  (1/2 to 1 cm) strips

Salt and freshly ground black
  pepper, to taste

2 large oranges, juiced, about 1
  cup (250 ml), divided

1 small yellow onion, peeled and
  chopped

9 ounces (250 g) Arborio rice

1 orange, zested

4 cups (1 l) warm chicken or
  vegetable stock or broth

2 tablespoons chopped fresh
  basil or 2 teaspoons dried, or
  1 tablespoon finely chopped
  fresh sage leaves or 1 teaspoon
  dried

1 1/2 cups (190 g) young, tiny
  sweet peas, fresh or frozen

THIS CREAMY RISOTTO BRIMMING WITH TENDER GREEN PEAS
and toothsome orange-glazed shiitake mushrooms is a delicious side dish or
starter topped with freshly grated Parmesan cheese. But add crumbled feta,
sautéed cubes of tofu, chunks of chicken or shrimp, and it transforms into a
fabulous family meal.

Heat 1 tablespoon of each the butter and oil in a large skillet over medium-low
until just sizzling. Add the mushrooms and salt and pepper and cook, stirring, until
tender, 4–5 minutes, adding more oil if needed. Add 1/4 cup (65 ml) orange juice
and simmer for 3–5 minutes until the juice evaporates and the mushrooms are very
tender and glazed. Transfer the mushrooms to a bowl and set aside.

Add the remaining butter and oil to the skillet and return to the heat.
Add the onion and cook, stirring, for 3–4 minutes over medium heat until
softened, transparent, and just starting to turn golden. Add the rice and zest
and toss with the onions until all the grains are coated in oil. Cook for 1–2
minutes, stirring, until the rice becomes translucent. Add 2 ladles of stock
and cook, stirring constantly and gently, until the liquid is almost absorbed.
Continue cooking the risotto over medium heat, adding 2 ladles of stock at a
time, stirring constantly, allowing each addition of liquid to be almost absorbed
before adding more broth. When the rice has cooked for 10 minutes, add the
remaining juice and cook until the liquid is absorbed. Continue cooking the
rice, stirring, adding 2 ladles of broth at a time until the liquid is absorbed,
about another 10 minutes.

If using fresh peas, add them with the first addition of stock once the
orange juice is absorbed. Stir in the fresh or dried herbs at the same time.

When the rice has cooked for a total of 20 minutes, stir in the frozen
peas, if using, and the mushrooms. Add any remaining stock and cook,
stirring, until the liquid is absorbed and the rice is tender and creamy. This
should take 20–25 minutes total cooking time from the moment the rice is
added to the skillet. Taste, and add more salt or pepper if needed.

Remove from the heat and allow to sit for 10 minutes before stirring the
risotto. Transfer to a platter to serve.

Quinoa Salad with Oranges, Pecans, and Cranberries

Serves 4

SALAD

1 1/2 cups (10 ounces / 285 g) quinoa or grain blend of choice

1 cup (250 ml) vegetable stock

1 1/2 cups (375 ml) water

1/2 cup (125 ml) freshly squeezed orange juice

1/4 cup (65 ml) pomegranate or cranberry juice

1/4 cup (1 ounce / 28 g) dried cranberries

2 navel oranges, cut into supremes

1 cup seedless red or green grapes, sliced in half

2 tablespoons thinly sliced scallions, both white and lighter green parts

1/2 cup (2 ounces / 55 g) lightly toasted, coarsely chopped pecans

(continued)

I LOVE THE DENSE, CHEWY TEXTURE OF QUINOA as much as I love the slightly nutty taste. Orange, cranberry, and pecan is a classic—and a favorite—autumn combination, one you'll see pop up again and again come Thanksgiving and Christmas. What better way to bring them together than in this healthful salad with a bright savory-sweet dressing, first created by my friend Barb Kiebel for her blog, *Creative Culinary*. This is a great make-ahead dish for a light, tasty, satisfying lunch, as an accompaniment to any roasted meat, or the perfect holiday side dish. Blood oranges can replace the navels for additional color; the quinoa can be replaced with mixed grains or wild rice.

Salad

Place the quinoa in a medium saucepan with the vegetable stock, water, and orange juice; bring to a boil. Reduce heat to low and simmer, covered, until the liquid has been absorbed, about 20 minutes; alternately, follow cooking directions for grain blend. Remove saucepan from heat, fluff the grains with a fork, cover, and let rest for 5 minutes. Remove the lid and allow to cool.

While the quinoa is cooking, warm the pomegranate juice in a small saucepan; remove from heat, add the cranberries, and soak in the warm juice to plump.

Once the quinoa has cooled, drain the cranberries, reserving the juice, and add the quinoa and cranberries to a large bowl along with the orange sections, grapes, scallions, and pecans; toss gently together to blend.

(continued)

DRESSING

1/2 cup (125 ml) olive oil

2 tablespoons freshly squeezed
lemon juice

1/4 cup (65 ml) raspberry or
balsamic vinegar

4 tablespoons honey

2 tablespoons Cointreau, Grand
Marnier, or orange juice

Reserved pomegranate juice

1/2 teaspoon salt

1/2 teaspoon freshly ground black
pepper

Dressing

Whisk together the oil, lemon juice, vinegar, honey, Cointreau, the reserved juice from the cranberries, salt, and pepper until well-blended. Drizzle half the dressing over the quinoa salad and stir in gently. Allow to sit for 30 minutes for the flavors to blend. Check seasonings and serve at room temperature with the rest of the dressing on the side.

Orange and Brown Sugar-Glazed Sweet Potatoes

Serves 4

4 medium whole sweet potatoes, unpeeled

2 oranges, juiced, about 3/4 cup (185 ml)

1 orange, zested

5 tablespoons (2.6 ounces / 75 g) unsalted butter

1/4 cup (1.8 ounces / 50 g) dark brown sugar

2 to 3 tablespoons lightly toasted flaked coconut or slivered almonds, for garnish, optional

REPLACE YOUR EVERYDAY POTATOES OR YOUR USUAL holiday sweet potato casserole with mouthwatering sweet potato wedges glazed in orange juice and brown sugar. Add a bit more warmth and complexity to this delicious side dish by adding a pinch of cinnamon or a grinding of black pepper to the pan while it cooks. The glazed potatoes can be cooked ahead of time and gently reheated over low heat, basting the potatoes as they warm, just before serving.

Cook the sweet potatoes in boiling water until they can be easily pierced through to the center with a fork or skewer, 25–35 minutes depending on the size of the potatoes. Remove the potatoes from the water, drain, and when cool enough to handle, peel and trim the ends. Cut each potato into 8 equal-size lengthwise wedges.

Heat the juice, zest, butter, and sugar in a skillet wide enough to hold all of the potato wedges in 1 layer. When the butter has melted and the mixture has come to a simmer, add the potatoes, making sure that they are mostly submerged in the liquid, and cook slowly over low heat, basting frequently, until the potatoes are glazed and the liquid has reduced to a thick sauce, 15–20 minutes.

Serve immediately topped with flaked coconut or slivered almonds.

Fruited Shrimp and Grilled Orange Quinoa Salad

Serves 2

Olive oil, for grilling

1 large orange

1 ripe pear, sliced

2 ripe figs, quartered

2 cups (9 ounces / 260 g) cooked quinoa or your favorite grain blend

3 1/2 ounces (100 g) cooked shrimp

3 tablespoons chopped fresh flat-leaf parsley

1/4 red onion, peeled, thinly sliced, and separated into strips

3 to 4 tablespoons crumbled feta, goat, or bleu cheese

8 ripe cherries, pitted and halved, and/or 2 tablespoons dried berries

3 tablespoons very good quality olive oil, plus more to taste

1 1/2 tablespoons balsamic or raspberry vinegar, plus more to taste

2 tablespoons orange juice, plus more to taste

Freshly ground black pepper, to taste

Salt, to taste

1/2 avocado or more, sliced lengthwise into 6 to 8 wedges

THIS IS A FLAVORFUL, HEALTHY SALAD, which I make for Jean-Pierre and myself anytime we crave something cool and fresh, even in the middle of winter, especially in orange season. I start with tender, nutty quinoa or a chewier quinoa-grain blend then add whatever I have on hand—steamed, grilled, or precooked shrimp, crumbly feta, bleu, or goat cheese, red onion, and seasonal fresh fruit. I'll mix in ripe figs or pears in the cooler months, cherries, blueberries, raspberries, or peaches in spring and summer, and toss in dried cranberries, blueberries, or cherries along with nuts or seeds for another great layer of flavor, a fantastic crunch, and a punch of nutrients. Even black olives would work.

Quantities of this salad can be easily increased and adapted, whether you simply want to add more of one ingredient and less of another or whether you are making salad for two, a family, or a party.

Brush a stovetop grill with oil and heat over medium to medium-high heat. Peel the orange, removing the white pith, and cut into 6 slices. Carefully place the orange slices on the hot grill. Allow to cook until softened just a bit and grill marks appear. Carefully flip the oranges and grill on the other side before removing to a plate. This should only take a few minutes. You can also grill the pear and figs if you like.

Place warm, cooked quinoa into a mixing bowl; add the shrimp, parsley, onion, cheese, and cherries. In a separate bowl, whisk together the oil, vinegar, orange juice, pepper, and salt, and drizzle over the salad. Toss to coat and adjust seasonings if needed.

Divide the salad between 2 plates. Place grilled orange, pear, figs, and avocado around or on the salads and serve.

Two Savory Orange Salads

3 medium or large oranges (juice, navel, or a mix)

1 large handful black or purple herb-marinated olives

Salt and freshly ground black pepper, to taste

Very good quality extra virgin olive oil

Sicilian Orange Salad

Serves 4

MY FRIEND, PHOTOGRAPHER ILVA BERETTA, is a Swede living in Tuscany, Italy, for almost as long as I've lived in France, more than twenty years, and she is a marvelous cook. She brings her Swedish love of simplicity and purity to the traditional Italian dishes she prepares for her family, using the best-quality local, seasonal ingredients, making sure the flavor of each of the few ingredients she combines in each dish shines. Her Sicilian Orange Salad cannot be any simpler, but it is sublime and refreshing, a wonderful first course for a meal eaten al fresco.

Scrub the outside of the oranges then thinly slice; alternately, peel the oranges, removing the skin and white pith, and slice into thin rounds. Evenly distribute the orange slices onto 4 salad plates. Top with olives, lightly season with salt and pepper, and then add a thin drizzle of oil. Leave to marinate at room temperature for about 10 minutes before serving.

3 medium or large oranges (juice, navel, or a mix)

1 large handful Niçoise or Greek olives

1 lemon, halved

Salt and freshly ground black pepper, to taste

Ground cumin, to taste

Smoked paprika, to taste

Very good quality extra virgin olive oil

Moroccan Orange Salad

Serves 4

MY HUSBAND, JEAN-PIERRE, spent two years living, working, and learning to cook in Casablanca and Rabat before we married. He introduced me to Moroccan cuisine, teaching me to cook with the flavors and spices of that warm, exotic country. Cumin, coriander, ras el hanout, preserved lemons, dates, almonds, and honey infuse so many Moroccan dishes with the same earthy, savory-sweet complexity found in this ambrosial Moroccan Orange Salad, a wonderful beginning to a North African meal, followed by a couscous or tagine.

Peel the oranges, removing the skin and white pith, and slice into thin rounds. Evenly distribute the orange slices onto 4 salad plates. Add a light squeeze of lemon juice over the orange slices and dust lightly with salt and pepper, cumin, and paprika. Top evenly with the olives and a thin drizzle of olive oil. Leave to marinate at room temperature for about 10 minutes before serving.

Orange-Braised Belgian Endives with Caramelized Onions and Bacon

Serves 2 to 4 as a side dish

2 small juice oranges

1/2 red or yellow onion

2 medium or 4 small Belgian endives

2 tablespoons olive oil, divided

2 to 3 tablespoons smoked lardons, or 3 to 4 strips smoky bacon, cut into small pieces

1/4 cup (65 ml) water

1/4 teaspoon honey

Salt and freshly ground black pepper, to taste

BRAISED BELGIAN ENDIVES ARE A COMMON SIDE DISH on French tables, done simply, caramelized in butter then bathed in water and cooked until tender. Searing gently caramelizes the endives, braising in orange juice tames the bitter bite leaving just a hint of piquancy that marries well with the sweetness of the orange and the smoky, salty finishing touch of the caramelized onion and the lardons or bacon. This is such a delectable accompaniment to roasted lamb or pork chops, grilled or pan-seared meats or fish, served along with roasted or steamed potatoes or carrots. You can omit the lardons or bacon for a meat-free side dish; instead, top the finished dish with some crumbled bleu cheese just before serving.

Using a vegetable peeler, pare off 2 long, wide strips of orange peel, avoiding the bitter white pith. Juice the oranges for $3/4$ cup (185 ml) liquid. Peel and thinly slice the onion. Remove and discard any damaged outer leaves from the endives and slice each in half lengthwise from top to bottom.

Heat 1 $1/2$ tablespoons oil over medium-low heat in a large skillet wide enough to comfortably hold all of the endive halves in 1 layer. Add the onion, separating the slices into strips, and cook, stirring, for 3 minutes or until soft and translucent. Lower the heat slightly if necessary to prevent scorching.

Add the lardons and continue cooking, stirring, for 3–4 minutes until cooked and beginning to brown (if using bacon, the bacon should be crispy) and the onion shrunken, very soft, and caramelized. Remove the onions and lardons from the pan and set aside.

(continued)

Add remaining $^1/_2$ tablespoon of oil to the pan and place the endives cut side down. Cook the endives in the oil for about 6 minutes, turning every 1–2 minutes, until tender and lightly seared and caramelized on all sides. Cook for an extra 1–2 minutes if needed. Lower the heat.

Remove the pan from the heat and add the 2 strips of peel and the orange juice; be careful as the juice will bubble up quickly. Once the bubbles calm down, return the pan to the heat and cook the endives in the orange juice for 6–8 minutes at a low boil. Continue to turn the endives every 1–2 minutes for even cooking.

When the juice has reduced to a syrup, add the water and stir in the honey; salt and pepper very lightly. Cook for a few more minutes until the liquid has reduced to a thick syrup just beginning to caramelize and the endives are very tender. Add the onions with the lardons back to the pan just to heat through. Remove and discard the strips of peel, and serve immediately.

Curly Kale and Pears with Orange Blossom Water

Serves 2

6 large leaves curly kale

1 medium onion, thinly sliced into rounds

1 to 2 tablespoons olive oil

1 teaspoon coconut oil or butter

1 tablespoon whole brown mustard seeds

2 small or 1 large underripe pears

1 to 2 cloves garlic, thinly sliced

1/4 teaspoon table, kosher, or sea salt

1/4 teaspoon cayenne or chipotle chili powder

2 tablespoons orange blossom water

2 teaspoons rice vinegar

THIS RECIPE CAN BE PREPARED IN ADVANCE and reheated at the last minute over low heat. Be sure to never cover the pan when it is on the stove, or the kale may get mushy.

Rinse the kale and, without shaking the kale dry, coarsely chop both the leaves and the stems into bite-size pieces, reserving them separately. Separate the onion slices into rings.

Pour the olive and coconut oils into a skillet and place over medium heat. Add the mustard seeds and, without stirring, leave them to sit until they begin to pop.

When the seeds start popping, add the onion and stir to coat with oil and mustard seeds. Cook, stirring occasionally, until soft and translucent, about 5 minutes. While the onion is cooking, core the unpeeled pears and cut into bite-size chunks.

When the onions are soft and translucent, add the garlic and kale stems and stir to blend and coat; sauté for 5 minutes. Stir in the pears and the wet chopped kale leaves. Add the salt and cayenne. Stir gently, making sure that all the leaves are coated with oil.

As the kale begins to wilt, add the orange blossom water and vinegar. Allow the vegetables to cook, uncovered, stirring occasionally, until the kale is no longer crunchy but still toothsome. Taste to adjust seasonings. Serve hot.

Gingered Orange Vichy Carrots

18 ounces (510 g) medium-size
carrots

2 tablespoons (1 ounce / 30 g)
unsalted butter

1 teaspoon granulated white
sugar

1 orange, finely zested and juiced,
about 1/2 cup (125 ml)

1 rounded tablespoon diced
candied crystallized ginger

1/8 teaspoon salt

Freshly ground black pepper,
to taste

1 cup (250 ml) water, plus more
if needed

1 to 2 tablespoons chopped fresh
flat-leaf parsley or cilantro, or
a pinch ground cumin to serve,
optional

A VERY OLD, VERY CLASSIC FRENCH DISH, sweet-glazed Vichy carrots, or *carottes à la Vichy*, was said to have been invented in the kitchens of the famed thermal station in the resort town of Vichy in central France sometime in the sixteenth century, local Vichy carrots were cooked in Vichy Saint-Yorre mineral water and Vichy salt. I've upped the game by glazing the carrots in orange juice, adding a subtle but delicious candy flavor to the sugar glaze, and some of the usual sugar is replaced with candied crystallized ginger, which adds a hint of the exotic, without the ginger coming on too strong. Vichy carrots, slick and shiny, sweet and toothsome, traditionally accompany veal cutlets or chops, sautéed or roasted chicken or meats, or simply prepared fish.

Trim and peel the carrots then slice into coins no thicker than 1/2 inch (1 cm); slice on the angle for a prettier presentation. Heat the butter, sugar, and zest in a wide skillet or sauté pan, stirring, until the butter has melted; add the carrots, ginger, salt, and pepper and cook, stirring and tossing the carrots, for 2 minutes. Add the orange juice and water; the carrots should be just covered with liquid. Bring to a boil, lower the heat, and simmer for 30 minutes, or until the carrots are tender and the sauce is reduced to a syrup. Be very careful not to let the carrots or the glaze burn; stir and toss the carrots occasionally.

At the end of 30 minutes, if the carrots are not as tender as you like, add an additional 1/4 cup (65 ml) water and cook for 15 more minutes.

Serve the carrots with a sprinkling of chopped parsley, or a pinch of ground cumin sprinkled just before serving.

NOTE: To serve 6 to 8, double all ingredients except the water, using only enough to cover the carrots.

Spiced Saffron Rice
with Barberries

Serves 4

1/2 teaspoon saffron threads

1 1/4 cups (375 ml) plus 2 cups
    (500 ml) water, divided

1 cup (6 1/2 ounces / 185 g)
    basmati rice

3 tablespoons olive oil, butter,
    or ghee

1 clove garlic, finely minced

2 oranges, finely zested

3 tablespoons barberries or dried
    sour cherries, blueberries, or
    cranberries

1/4 teaspoon ground cardamom

1 teaspoon salt

2 teaspoons smoked paprika or
    Aleppo pepper

1 cup (250 ml) orange juice

THIS WARMLY SPICED RICE WITH A TOUCH OF SWEET FRUIT
is a riff on a pilaf or polow, a Persian or Indian dish in which rice is cooked in
seasoned broth. Pair it with marinated grilled meats or fish, or a spicy dish,
whether an Indian or Pakistani meal.

Place the saffron in 1 1/4 cups (375 ml) water and set aside to steep.

Bring the 2 cups (500 ml) water to a boil in a medium saucepan and stir
in the rice. Bring the water back up to a boil and boil for 30 seconds; drain the
rice in a fine colander and rinse thoroughly with cool water. Set aside.

Heat the oil over medium heat in a large saucepan. Add the garlic, zest,
barberries, cardamom, salt, and paprika. Cook, stirring, for 1–2 minutes.

Add the saffron water, orange juice, and rice. Bring to a boil, turn down
the heat to a simmer, and cook, covered, for 15–20 minutes. Uncover the pot
for the last few minutes and stir the rice as it finishes cooking, adding up to
1/4 cup (65 ml) more water if the rice isn't yet tender and needs a few more
minutes to cook. Remove from heat and fluff rice with a fork. Cover to keep
warm until ready to serve.

Main
Dishes

Oven-Baked Stuffed Chicken with Orange-Soy Gravy

Serves 4 to 6

3 sweet oranges

2 cloves garlic

1 (4- to 5-pound /1.8 to 2.25 kg) whole chicken

Salt and freshly ground black pepper, to taste

1/2 teaspoon Orange Powder (page 19), optional

1/4 cup (65 ml) soy sauce

1/4 teaspoon ground ginger or 1 teaspoon finely grated fresh ginger

1/2 teaspoon allspice

1 tablespoon dark brown sugar

1 tablespoon cornstarch dissolved in 2 tablespoons water

2 tablespoons Cointreau or Grand Marnier

1/2 to 1 tablespoon honey

WHY JUST BAKE A CHICKEN when you can serve the same chicken with warm orange chunks and topped with a flavorful gravy? Soy, orange, and Cointreau blend beautifully, creating a full-flavored savory sauce without one of the individual components overpowering the others. Chilled, any leftover sauce gels and makes a delicious condiment for a chicken sandwich.

Preheat oven to 350 degrees F (180 degrees C). Finely zest 2 of the oranges, reserving zest. Peel the zested oranges, removing the rind and white pith; slice and cube the fruit. Juice the remaining orange for about 1/2 cup (125 ml) juice; set aside. Crush 1 clove garlic and mince the other clove.

Pat the chicken dry inside and out. Rub the inside and outside of the chicken with the crushed garlic, salt and pepper, and dust with the Orange Powder. Place the orange cubes into the cavity of the bird and place the chicken, breast side up, snugly in a baking dish. Press the zest into the skin of the chicken, all over the breast, legs, and thighs; alternately, you can push the zest under the skin.

Lightly whisk together the orange juice, soy sauce, ginger, allspice, brown sugar, and minced garlic and pour into the baking dish around the chicken. Bake for 1 1/2–1 3/4 hours, until the skin is golden brown and crispy and the inside meat temperature reads 165 degrees F (75 degrees C) on a baking thermometer.

Remove from the oven and place the chicken on a serving dish; if you like, pull apart or cut the chicken into pieces, first scooping out the orange chunks into a serving bowl. Pour the cooking liquid into a saucepan over medium heat and bring to a boil. Whisk in the cornstarch mixture and Cointreau. Cook for about 10 minutes on a low boil until thickened. Add the honey, stir, and taste, adding more honey and adjusting the seasoning if desired.

Serve the chicken accompanied by the orange chunks and the sauce with white or wild rice, pasta, or crushed potatoes. You can also shred the chicken, drizzle with sauce, and top with orange chunks and pomegranate seeds.

Sweet-and-Sour Marmalade-Glazed Oven-Baked Chicken

Serves 6

2 tablespoons vegetable oil

2 large shallots, chopped

1/2 teaspoon ground ginger

1/2 cup (125 ml) white wine vinegar

2/3 cup (150 ml) light soy sauce

1 cup (12 1/2 ounces / 350 g) orange marmalade

1/4 teaspoon salt

1/4 teaspoon freshly ground black pepper

1 large whole chicken, cut into pieces, or 6 bone-in, skin-on chicken thighs and legs

I LOVE SWEET AND SOUR OR SAVORY AND SWEET DISHES, and I adore fruit with meat. With this dish I have all three and it couldn't be easier. All I have to do is marinate the chicken overnight and then just pop it in the oven, prepare a side dish while it's baking—rice topped with grilled, roasted, or sautéed vegetables in the summer, potato pancakes in the winter, or simply a big mixed salad—and I have a perfect meal.

Using either bitter or sweet orange marmalade will make for a delicious marinade, but bitter will definitely give this dish some oomph and a more pronounced personality. Use marmalade that has more jelly than rind, but do make sure there is rind in it to give the glaze that delicious bitter edge. This chicken is delicious eaten hot, at room temperature, or even as leftovers straight from the refrigerator, and it would even make great picnic fare.

Heat the oil in a medium saucepan, and cook the shallots over medium heat until soft and golden, 3–5 minutes. Stir in the ginger until dissolved then stir in the vinegar and boil vigorously until reduced by half, 2–3 minutes.

Add the soy sauce, marmalade, salt, and pepper and stir until smooth and the jam has dissolved. As soon as the marinade comes to a boil, lower the heat and simmer, stirring occasionally, for 15 minutes. Remove from heat and allow to cool to room temperature.

Rinse and pat the chicken pieces dry, removing excess skin and fat pockets. Place chicken in a wide shallow bowl or a large sealable plastic bag. Pour the cooled marinade over the chicken, making sure the pieces are completely submerged. Cover the bowl tightly with plastic wrap, or seal the plastic bag tightly. Place in the refrigerator for several hours, or overnight.

When ready to cook, preheat oven to 425 degrees F (220 degrees C). Prepare a large, shallow baking pan by lining it with aluminum foil, overlapping 2 extra-strong pieces of foil and folding over two or three times then pressing the seam flat. Oil the foil to keep the cooked chicken from sticking. Arrange the chicken in 1 layer in the pan then spoon the marinade over the pieces. To avoid having too much marinade pooling in the bottom of the pan, spoon some over the chicken and spoon or brush more over the chicken once or twice during baking.

Bake for 35–45 minutes, until cooked through and beautifully glazed and browned. Keep an eye on the chicken toward the end of the baking time, as the marmalade will go from crispy to burned in a matter of minutes.

While the chicken is baking, place the remaining marinade in a small saucepan and simmer over low heat until reduced to $1/2$ to $2/3$ cup (125 to 170 ml) and thickened.

NOTE: For a wonderful variation on this recipe, prepare the marinade as indicated and set aside. Pan fry bone-in pork or lamb chops in olive oil. When the chops are done to your liking, remove them from the skillet to a plate and deglaze the skillet with a couple of tablespoons of sherry or orange juice, scraping up any brown bits stuck to the bottom. Lower the heat under the pan, add the marinade and simmer until reduced and thickened, and then spoon over the chops to serve.

Orange Rosemary Wedding Day Chicken

Serves 4 to 6

1 (4-pound / 1.8 kg) chicken cut into pieces, or the equivalent in pieces of choice

1 cup (250 ml) orange juice

1 lemon, juiced and zested

6 (3-inch) sprigs fresh rosemary, divided

3/4 cup (3 1/2 ounces / 100 g) all-purpose flour

1 teaspoon salt

1/2 teaspoon freshly ground black pepper

1 teaspoon smoked paprika

1/4 cup (65 ml) vegetable oil, divided, for frying

1/4 cup (65 ml) chicken stock

1/2 small orange, juiced

1/2 lemon, juiced

1 tablespoon light brown sugar

1 tablespoon grated orange zest

1 small orange, sliced paper thin

ORANGE ROSEMARY CHICKEN WAS THE MAIN COURSE at my wedding lunch, the centerpiece of a perfect rustic meal prepared by myself and Jean-Pierre. Marinating the chicken in the juice infuses the meat with citrusy flavor while tenderizing it. Frying the seasoned chicken before baking gives it a beautiful crispy outside, and baking it makes the dish so easy. This dish is as delicious cold as it is hot and is ideal—if messy—to take along on a picnic. Serve over rice, pilaf, or grains.

Rinse and pat the chicken pieces dry, removing excess skin and fat pockets. Place the chicken, orange juice, and juice from the whole lemon in a glass bowl just large enough to hold the chicken comfortably; reserve the lemon zest. Mince the leaves of 2 of the sprigs of rosemary and add to the marinade. Cover tightly with plastic wrap and refrigerate overnight, turning occasionally.

When ready to cook, drain the chicken pieces. Put the flour, salt, pepper, and paprika in a large bowl or plastic bag and mix thoroughly. Working in batches, lightly coat 1 to 2 pieces of chicken at a time in the seasoned flour, shaking off excess. Set the chicken aside on a clean, dry plate.

Heat half of the oil in a large skillet or Dutch oven. When the oil is very hot, fry the chicken pieces, a few at a time so as not to overcrowd, on all sides, until well-browned and crispy. This may take up to 10 minutes per batch. Add the rest of the oil to the pan as needed.

Preheat oven to 350 degrees F (180 degrees C).

Arrange the browned chicken in a single layer in a large, shallow baking dish. Pour the stock around the pieces, not filling the dish more than halfway up the sides of the chicken, then add the juice of the 1/2 orange and 1/2 lemon into the stock. Sprinkle the chicken evenly with the brown sugar and orange and lemon zests. Place remaining sprigs of rosemary into the liquid around the chicken and set a thin slice of orange on each piece of chicken. Bake for about 45 minutes, or until cooked through to the bone and tender.

Beef in Bourbon Sauce

Serves 4

1 tablespoon all-purpose flour

1 teaspoon Orange Powder
(page 19)

1/4 teaspoon salt

1/4 teaspoon freshly ground black
pepper

28 ounces (800 g) stewing
beef, such as marbled chuck,
shoulder, roast, or sirloin, cut
into 8 or so large chunks

1 tablespoon margarine or butter

1 tablespoon or more olive oil

2 medium yellow onions, diced

2 cloves garlic, coarsely chopped
or diced

2 wide strips of peel from
1 orange

1/3 cup (85 ml) bourbon

3/4 cup (180 ml) orange juice

1/4 cup (65 ml) soy sauce

3 tablespoons honey

1 orange, finely zested

1/2 teaspoon ground ginger
or 1-inch cube fresh ginger,
peeled and grated

1/4 teaspoon ground allspice

1 pound (450 g) carrots, peeled,
trimmed, and sliced into 3/4-
to 1-inch (2 to 3 cm) coins

Salt and freshly ground black
pepper, to taste

BEEF IN BOURBON SAUCE IS A SUCCULENT, richly flavored dish, at once homey and elegant, perfect for a winter meal or a dinner party. Serve over grains, wild rice, or wide, flat noodles. This is even more delicious reheated the following day; simply add water when reheating to keep from burning.

Mix the flour, Orange Powder, salt, and pepper together on a large dinner plate or in a wide, shallow soup dish. Toss the beef in the seasoned flour, pressing to coat all sides of each cube. You can also do this in a large sealable plastic bag.

Heat the margarine and oil over medium-high heat in a large, heavy pot or Dutch oven wide enough to hold the beef in a single layer. When the fat is hot and begins to sizzle, add the beef and lightly brown on all sides, 4–5 minutes. Add the onions, garlic, orange peels, and any remaining seasoned flour and cook, stirring until the onions are tender and the meat is nicely browned, about 5 minutes.

Carefully lift the beef out of the pot and place on a plate. Lower the heat slightly and add the bourbon to deglaze the pot, scraping up any browned bits sticking to the bottom. Heat the bourbon for just 2 minutes to allow the alcohol to burn off.

Stir the orange juice, soy sauce, honey, zest, ginger, and allspice together in a small bowl and add to the pot; return the beef to the pot. Add enough water to barely, but not quite, cover the meat. Once the sauce has come to a boil, lower the heat, cover the pot, and allow to slowly simmer for 1 1/2 hours, adding more water only as needed so the sauce doesn't reduce too much; the meat should remain a bit more than half submerged in sauce.

After cooking for 1 1/2 hours, add the carrots, a bit more water if needed, and continue cooking, covered, for an additional 45 minutes, or until the carrots are tender. Remove the lid for the last 10 minutes of cooking if the sauce needs to reduce. The meat and the carrots should be beautifully tender and glazed, and the liquid reduced to a thickened sauce. Taste and adjust the seasonings, and add water to thin the sauce if desired.

NOTE: You can easily adapt this recipe for use in your slow cooker: brown the seasoned, floured beef cubes in a skillet with the onion. Transfer to the slow cooker, deglaze the skillet with the bourbon, add the remaining ingredients, and cook on high for 2 1/2 hours, and then low for another 2 hours. Add a bit of cornstarch to thicken 30 minutes before the end of cooking.

Mediterranean Lamb or Veal Meatballs

Serves 4 to 6

MEATBALLS

1 cup soft fresh breadcrumbs from crustless sandwich bread

3 tablespoons orange juice

20 to 25 ounces (560 to 700 g) ground lamb, veal, or half each lamb and beef

1 large egg, slightly beaten

4 tablespoons finely chopped fresh cilantro (coriander) or flat-leaf parsley, plus more, for garnish

1 large clove garlic, peeled and finely minced

1 teaspoon salt

1/2 teaspoon freshly ground black pepper

1/4 teaspoon smoked paprika

1/4 teaspoon ground coriander or cumin

1 teaspoon orange zest or Orange Powder (page 19)

1 tablespoon vegetable or olive oil

(continued)

ORANGES, LEMONS, AND LOADS OF FRESH AND DRIED spices give this dish a bright, distinctive Mediterranean twist to your everyday meatballs in red sauce, whether using lamb, veal, or beef. Have everything prepared, measured, weighed, chopped, minced, and zested before starting the recipe. I added mild dried ñora peppers, which infuse the sauce with an intriguing hint of sweet and smoky, but the sauce is just as delicious without the peppers.

Meatballs

Place the breadcrumbs in a shallow soup bowl and add the orange juice; toss until the bread has soaked up the juice.

Place the ground meat in a large mixing bowl; add the softened breadcrumbs and all the remaining meatball ingredients except the oil. Using your hands, squeeze and combine until well-blended. Shape into 20 to 25 well-packed meatballs, about 1 1/2–1 3/4-inches (about 4 cm) diameter. Heat the oil in a large skillet on medium-high heat; add the meatballs and sear on all sides until browned and crispy on the outside, 4–5 minutes. If cooking the meatballs in 2 batches, add a bit more oil to the pan for the second batch, if needed. Remove browned meatballs from the pan and reserve on a plate.

(continued)

1 tablespoon vegetable or olive oil

1 medium yellow onion, chopped

2 medium cloves garlic, thinly sliced

1 cup (250 ml) dry white wine

1/2 cup (125 ml) orange juice

1/4 cup (65 ml) lemon juice

1 tablespoon orange zest

1 1/2 cups (13 ounces / 370 g) canned chopped tomatoes with the liquid

3 tablespoons tomato purée

1 bay leaf

1 teaspoon crushed fennel or anise seeds

3 teaspoons minced fresh oregano or 1 1/2 teaspoons dried

3 teaspoons minced fresh thyme or lemon thyme, or 1 1/2 teaspoons dried

2 tablespoons coarsely chopped fresh basil

1 to 2 whole dried ñora peppers, split in half to the stem, seeds removed, optional

Salt and freshly ground black pepper, to taste

Freshly grated Parmesan cheese, for garnish

Sauce

Lower the heat to medium and add oil to the skillet. Add the onion and garlic and sauté for 3–5 minutes until soft. Add the wine to deglaze the pan, scraping up the brown bits from the bottom, and let the wine boil for 1 minute. Whisk all of the remaining sauce ingredients together in a small bowl, except for the Parmesan, until well-mixed. Add to the skillet, stir well, lower the heat slightly, and simmer uncovered, stirring occasionally, until the sauce is slightly thickened, 4–5 minutes. Taste and add more salt and pepper as desired.

Slide the meatballs into the sauce and simmer, stirring occasionally, until cooked through, about 10 minutes depending on the size of the meatballs and how well you like them cooked.

Serve hot with pasta, topped with fresh cilantro and Parmesan cheese.

VARIATION: Another great way to serve these meatballs is to spoon them on top of toasted pain de campagne or into a split roll and cover in sauce, dusted with fresh herbs and Parmesan.

The sauce is also delicious with fish. Either simmer 4 thin 4-ounce (115 g) rockfish, sole, flounder, or cod fillets in the sauce, or pop it all into a 375-degree F (190 degrees C) oven for 15 minutes.

Breaded Veal Chops
with Orange, Tomato,
and Red Onion Salsa

VEAL CHOPS

1 medium juicy orange

2 medium-thick veal chops

1/8 cup (20 g) all-purpose flour

1/4 teaspoon salt

Freshly ground black pepper,
   to taste

1 large egg

1/2 cup (1.6 ounces / 45 g) fine
   dry breadcrumbs, preferably
   homemade, or herbed
   breadcrumbs

1/2 teaspoon fresh thyme leaves

(continued)

WHETHER YOU LOVE FRYING OR GRILLING or prefer the lightness and freshness of oven baking, everyone loves chops, tender and juicy, enveloped in crispy, tasty breading. This recipe is fabulous with veal, pork, or lamb chops and works beautifully whether frying, grilling, or baking. The meat and the breading are infused with the delicate flavors of orange and thyme and the salsa adds fruitiness and a tart tang to the dish. The oven-baked breaded chops are simple to make, quick to bake, and the result is everything we love without the greasiness or the heaviness of frying. But go ahead and pan sear the chops in a little olive oil or grill on high until seared then lower the heat and finish cooking to your taste.

Veal Chops

Preheat oven to 400 degrees F (200 degrees C).

Finely grate the orange and set the zest aside. Slice the orange in half and juice 1 half. Remove the peel, white pith, and white spongy core of the remaining orange half. Dice the fruit, reserving any runoff juice, and place the fruit in a bowl. Set aside for use in the salsa.

Place the juice of the squeezed half orange into a wide, shallow bowl large enough to comfortably, but snugly, hold the chops in a single layer. Add the chops, turning each over until coated with juice. Allow the chops to marinate in the juice while you prepare the ingredients for the breading and the salsa, turning them once or twice.

(continued)

1 small ripe tomato, cored and
chopped

1/4 red onion, peeled and diced

2 teaspoons chopped fresh
cilantro (coriander), or more
to taste

Reserved diced orange

1 teaspoon olive oil

1/4 to 1/2 teaspoon fresh
squeezed lime or lemon juice,
or to taste

Salt and freshly ground black
pepper, to taste

Season the flour with salt and a healthy grinding of black pepper and place on a large plate or in a wide soup bowl. Lightly beat the egg in a large, shallow soup bowl, whisking in any reserved orange juice from the diced orange. Blend the breadcrumbs, zest, and thyme until well combined on a large plate or wide soup bowl.

Lift the chops from the juice and shake off excess liquid. Dip each chop into the flour, coating both sides, shaking off any excess. Dip each floured chop into the egg mixture, letting the excess run back into the bowl, and then finally dip each chop into the breadcrumbs making sure both sides are well coated.

Place the breaded chops on a lightly greased baking sheet or on a lightly greased grill rack sitting on a baking sheet, and bake until the breading is golden and crispy and the chops are cooked through, as pink or as white as you like, 10–20 minutes depending on your oven and the size and thickness of your chops.

Once the veal chops are baked to desired doneness and the outside is golden, serve immediately topped with some of the salsa.

Orange, Tomato, and Red Onion Salsa

To prepare the salsa, add the tomato, onion, and cilantro to the diced orange; mix gently. Add the oil, lime juice, and a small pinch of both salt and pepper; toss to blend. Taste the salsa, adding more lime juice, salt, and/or pepper as desired. Set aside.

Zucchini and Spinach Quiche with Orange, Dates, Feta, and Thyme

Serves 8 to 10

ORANGE SAVORY PASTRY CRUST

1 3/4 cups (8.3 ounces / 235 g) all-purpose flour

3/4 teaspoon salt or Orange Salt (page 22)

1 small or medium orange, finely zested

12 tablespoons (6 ounces / 170 g) cold unsalted butter, cubed

4 to 6 tablespoons cold orange juice or water

(continued)

THIS SAVORY-SWEET QUICHE IS THE PERFECT brunch food, an egg and cream-rich filling with a hint of orange and herbs. It's chock-full of baby spinach, grilled zucchini, and tangy feta cheese and made extra special with the sweetness of oranges and dates all in a delicate pastry shell. Satisfying, comforting, and healthy, this quiche is sure to please your favorite vegetarians, but don't hesitate, if you choose, to layer in shredded smoked salmon or crumbled, crispy-fried smoky bacon. Delicious served hot, warm, room temperature, or chilled, this quiche is ideal for a buffet or a picnic as well as a light lunch.

Orange Savory Pastry Crust

You will need a 10 x 1 1/2-inch (24 x 2.5 cm) deep pie or quiche dish.

Place the flour, salt, and zest in a large mixing bowl. Add the butter, tossing to coat with flour. Using the tips of your fingers and thumbs, rub the butter and flour together rapidly until the mixture is crumbly and resembles damp sand and the zest is no longer clumped but well dispersed. Do not overwork.

Add 4 tablespoons of juice and blend vigorously with a fork until all of the dry ingredients are moistened and the dough begins to pull together into a shaggy ball, adding more liquid only as needed.

(continued)

1 pound (450 g) slender zucchini

1 tablespoon olive oil

2 ounces (60 g) baby spinach

3 1/2 ounces (100 g) feta cheese

6 Medjool dates

1 cup bite-size orange cubes

1/4 cup (65 ml) orange juice

3/4 cup (185 ml) heavy or light cream, or half cream and half whole milk

3 large eggs

3/4 teaspoon salt or Orange Salt (page 22)

Freshly ground black pepper, to taste

1/8 teaspoon ground nutmeg

1 1/2 teaspoons chopped fresh thyme leaves, or 1/2 teaspoon dried thyme

1 orange, zested

2 tablespoons chopped hazelnuts

Scrape the dough out onto a floured work surface. With the heel of 1 hand, rapidly smear and push the dough onto the surface away from you to completely blend the butter and the flour together. Scrape the dough up and gather it into a ball. Knead gently and briefly, just enough to make a smooth, homogeneous ball of dough. Cover in plastic wrap and refrigerate until firm enough to roll out easily, about 15 minutes.

On a well-floured surface, roll the dough out into a circle about 1 inch (2 cm) or so larger than the pie dish. Gently lift and fit the dough into the dish, trimming off any excess dough from around the edge. Prick the bottom and sides of the dough with a fork and set aside at room temperature while you prepare the filling.

Quiche Filling

Set your oven on the grill/broiler setting and place the rack in the center of the oven.

Wash and trim the zucchini; cut each in half and then cut each half into long 1/4-inch-thick (1/2 cm) slices. Lay the slices on a parchment-lined baking sheet, brush each lightly with oil, and place in the oven for 10–15 minutes, until fork tender. Remove from the oven to cool.

Preheat oven to 375 degrees F (190 degrees C).

Snap off and discard any sharp or tough stems from the spinach and coarsely chop the leaves. Crumble the feta. Slice the dates into 4 to 5 pieces each, discarding the pits. Evenly spread the spinach, feta, zucchini, dates, and orange cubes in the prepared pie dish.

Whisk together the orange juice, cream, eggs, salt, pepper, nutmeg, thyme, and zest and pour into the dish. Scatter the hazelnuts evenly over the filling. Bake for 1 hour, or until the filling is puffed, set in the center, and beginning to turn golden and the pastry shell is a nice golden brown. Remove from the oven and allow to set for 15 minutes before serving.

Fish Tagine with Preserved Lemon, Olives, Orange, and Saffron

Serves 2

2 teaspoons ras el hanout, plus more

1 teaspoon Orange Powder (page 19)

Pinch of red adobo chili powder, plus more

2 (6-ounce / 170 g) thick codfish fillets or other dense white fish

2 tablespoons olive oil

1 small yellow onion, chopped

1 clove garlic, chopped

1 medium potato, peeled and cut into small cubes

1/2 zucchini, peeled and cut into small cubes

1/2 green bell pepper, seeds and ribs removed, chopped

1 small preserved lemon (*citron confit*), halved or quartered

2 tablespoons tiny dried sultanas

1 medium-large orange, cut into supremes

(continued)

THIS FISH TAGINE IS AS EXOTIC AND BEAUTIFUL as it is simple to make. The classic Moroccan tagine combination of preserved lemon and olives is this time paired with a plump, meaty, tender, and moist fish fillet. The orange adds a kiss of sweet to the delicately spiced sauce, and adding just a squeeze of Seville or Bergamot juice right before serving will add complexity to the sauce. The saffron adds a depth and a stunning color to the dish.

Soulful and satisfying, this is a dish for two that my husband learned to cook while living in Morocco that he makes for me on Valentine's Day. Serve over hot couscous, garnished with a bit of cilantro.

Combine the ras el hanout, Orange Powder, and chili powder in a small bowl. Rub the spice mixture on both sides of each fillet, adding more if you prefer a spicier flavor. Heat the oil in a large pot or Dutch oven over medium heat.

Once the oil is hot, add the onion and garlic; stir to coat. Add the fish skin side down to sear quickly, just 1–2 minutes; flip and sear the other side; you want the outside of the fish to color and shrink slightly but not to cook through. Carefully remove the fish from the pot, and place on a plate.

Add the potato, zucchini, bell pepper, lemon, sultanas, and orange supremes to the pot with just enough water to barely cover the vegetables. Add the salt and pepper, saffron, and a pinch more of the ras el hanout and chili powder and allow to simmer until the potatoes are tender, about 10 minutes; add water as needed so the potatoes remain submerged.

Water

Salt and freshly ground black
pepper, to taste

1/8 teaspoon saffron powder or
turmeric

2 tablespoons chopped fresh
cilantro (coriander), plus more
for garnish

1 cup purple or Niçoise olives

1 small bitter Seville or Bergamot
orange or 1 small sweet orange

Once all of the vegetables are tender, return the fish to the pot along with the olives, cilantro, and just a squeeze of bitter or sweet orange, if you like. Allow to simmer just until the fish fillets are cooked through, adding more water to keep the fillets not more than halfway submerged in the sauce. This should only take a few minutes. Taste the sauce and adjust the seasonings if necessary. Serve hot with more cilantro.

Curried Cod Poached in Coconut Milk, Lime, and Orange

Serves 4

COD

1 fresh mild green pepper such as a guindilla, Basque fryer, Guernica, or Anaheim, stem removed

1/2 cup (125 ml) lime juice from about 3 juicy limes

1/2 cup (125 ml) orange juice from 2 oranges

1 2/3 cups (400 ml) thick coconut milk or coconut cream

1 tablespoon mild or medium curry powder

2 to 3 tablespoons chopped fresh cilantro (coriander)

Salt and freshly ground black pepper, to taste

4 (6-ounce / 170 g) thick cod fillets

1 tablespoon butter

(continued)

MY SISTER-IN-LAW CATHERINE DECIDED TO MOVE HER FAMILY to Tahiti where they stayed for a year or two. Although they have been back in France for many years, the flavors and cuisine of this beautiful tropical island still infuse her cooking. On a recent visit with us, she prepared a simple dish of cod fillets poached in lime juice, coconut milk, and curry powder—just a few ingredients but incredibly flavorful.

This is my version. Any leftover rice and sauce can be mixed together, heated gently on medium-low heat and eaten with halved hardboiled eggs or steamed asparagus for a light meal.

Cod

Slice the pepper in half lengthwise and scrape out and discard the seeds. Slice each half into 2 lengthwise strips. Whisk together the lime juice, orange juice, coconut milk, curry powder, cilantro, and salt and pepper until blended.

Rinse the fillets and pat dry with paper towels. Lightly salt and pepper each fillet on both sides.

Heat a wok or a deep skillet over medium heat. Add the butter. When the butter melts and begins to sizzle, add the pepper slices and gently slide in the cod fillets and cook to sear quickly for 1 minute; flip and cook the other side for 1 minute. Pour the coconut milk mixture over the fish, covering completely. Once the liquid is heated through and starts to barely come to a boil, 1–2 minutes, lower the heat to medium-low and allow the fish to poach in the liquid just under a simmer for 3 minutes, or until just cooked through. Taste and add more salt, pepper, or orange juice as needed and desired.

(continued)

1 large yellow onion, peeled

1 tablespoon butter or margarine

1 tablespoon extra virgin olive oil

1 1/2 cups basmati or Thai rice

Salt and freshly ground black
    pepper, to taste

2 1/2 cups water

Chopped fresh cilantro
    (coriander), for garnish

Turn off the heat under the wok or skillet, letting the fish and sauce rest while you prepare the rice. When the rice is cooked and ready to serve, gently reheat the coconut milk sauce and fish to serving temperature. Place a ladleful of rice in each of 4 wide soup bowls, and top with a cod fillet and sauce. Sprinkle with fresh cilantro and pass the spoons.

Onion and Rice Pilaf

Quarter the onion and cut each quarter into $1/8$- to $1/4$-inch (about $1/2$ cm) slices, separating the layers.

Place the butter and oil in a large, deep skillet or sauté pan over medium-high heat. When the fat is melted and sizzling, add the onion. Cook, stirring, until the onion softens, 3–5 minutes.

Add the rice to the onions in the pan all at once, turn the heat down to medium, and stir to coat the grains with the butter and oil. Continue stirring as you cook the rice for 3–4 minutes, until the grains are glossy and starting to look transparent. Season well with salt and pepper.

Turn the heat down to low or medium-low and add the water, 1 or 2 ladles at a time. Cook the rice until the liquid is almost completely absorbed, stirring occasionally to keep the rice from burning, before adding another ladle or 2 of water. Continuing adding water and cook, stirring often, until all of the water is added and most of the liquid has been absorbed, about 15 minutes. Turn the heat to the lowest setting and let rest for 5–10 minutes before fluffing with a fork. Taste and add more salt and pepper as desired.

Whole Herb-Stuffed Sea Bream with Orange

Serves 4

Olive oil

2 medium to large oranges, preferably with thinner rind

1 (2-pound / 1 kg) whole sea bream, or 4 fish fillets of choice (about 1 pound / 450 g)

Salt and freshly ground black pepper, to taste

2 shallots, minced

2 cloves garlic, minced

1 small bunch flat-leaf parsley, leaves chopped

1 small bunch fresh cilantro (coriander), leaves chopped

1 teaspoon ground cumin

1/2 lemon, juiced

1/4 cup (65 ml) dry white wine

1/4 teaspoon fresh minced or dried thyme

THIS IS A SIMPLE WAY TO PREPARE FISH so that it always comes out of the oven tender and moist, while the juices and fresh herbs delicately flavor the flesh. If preparing the recipe with a whole fish, it should be gutted and scaled; ask your fishmonger to clean and prepare it for you if you prefer. You can replace the bream with sea bass or red snapper fillets and simply mound the herbs on top of the fillets or roll them around the filling.

Preheat oven to 425 degrees F (220 degrees C). Rub the bottom and sides of a baking dish large enough to hold the fish with oil.

Juice 1 of the oranges. Trim the top and bottom from the second orange, cut away the peel and white pith, and cut into supremes or slices. Reserve the supremes, squeeze out the juice from the remaining membranes, and discard.

Scale, empty, and clean the sea bream if not already done by your fishmonger. Rinse and pat dry with paper towels. Rub the outside of the fish with a bit more of the oil and season, inside and out, with salt and pepper. If using fillets, rinse and pat dry with paper towels and sprinkle lightly with salt and pepper.

Combine the shallots, garlic, parsley, cilantro, cumin, and a large pinch each of salt and pepper. Stuff all of the shallot-herb mixture into the cavity of the fish, pressing it in so the fish is well filled and all of the mixture is used. Close and secure the opening with toothpicks.

Drizzle 1 tablespoon of oil down the center of the baking pan; add the orange and lemon juices and wine. Scatter the orange supremes in the baking dish and place the stuffed fish on top of the fruit. If using fillets, place the fish in a single layer on top of the oranges and mound the filling on top of the fillets; alternately, roll the fillets around the filling, secure with toothpicks, and line up on top of the supremes. Sprinkle the fish with thyme.

Bake the fish for 30 minutes if using the whole fish, or 20 minutes for fillets, until just cooked through. Check the fish a few minutes early to avoid overcooking.

Serve with rice or grains, spooning some of the juices and orange segments over the fish.

Mussels Steamed in Orange and Fennel

Serves 4 as a main dish,
or 6 to 8 as a starter

4 1/2 pounds (2 kg) fresh mussels

2 large navel or juice oranges

1 small fennel bulb

3 to 4 tablespoons olive oil

4 small or 2 large shallots, chopped

1 large handful fresh flat-leaf parsley, chopped

Salt and freshly ground black pepper, to taste

1 cup (250 ml) white wine

GREMOLATA (GARNISH)

2 tablespoons pine nuts, optional

1 small orange

1 small lemon

2 tablespoons finely minced fresh flat-leaf parsley

BEFORE WE WERE MARRIED, MY SOON-TO-BE HUSBAND took my sister and me on a road trip, from Paris to Dieppe, to walk on the rain and windswept beach and then eat *moules frites*, the traditional local fare, in a little seaside bistro. Since then, my husband and I have cooked innumerable pots of *moules marinières*, marinated mussels steamed in white wine, in a variety of styles, and always served up with a customary platter of French fries.

The joy of cooking mussels is multifold: it is inexpensive, quick, and easy: it is a food rich in protein, iodine, iron, copper, and selenium as well as a good source of calcium; and it is so impressive on the table. Once you master the technique of steaming mussels, you can vary it to adapt to your taste and pantry, in cream sauce, with lemon or curry, with chopped fresh tomatoes, or in orange juice with the addition of the smoky anise-flavor of fennel. Just use a light, dry, fruity wine such as a Muscadet.

Pour the mussels into your sink and pick them over, removing and discarding any that are open or any with a crushed shell. The general rule to remember is that before cooking, discard all open mussels, and after cooking, discard any mussels that have remained closed.

To remove the mussel beard, grab the hairy strings hanging out of the closed shell and pull out and down, yanking sharply to pull it out of the mussel. Transfer the debearded mussels to a large colander. Run the mussels under cold running water, tossing and scrubbing, to wash off any sand and impurities.

Pare off 2 (1 x 3-inch /2 x 8 cm) strips of orange peel without the white pith, and then juice the 2 oranges. Trim off the stems of the fennel bulb, reserving about 1 tablespoon of the feathery fronds. Slice the fennel into long, thin strips or matchsticks.

Heat the oil in a very large pot with a lid. Add the shallots, fennel, and orange peels; cook over medium-high heat, stirring, for 3–5 minutes, until the fennel is tender and transparent. Add the fennel fronds, parsley, salt, and pepper. Add the mussels and, with a large slotted spoon, stir and toss to blend well. Pour the wine and the orange juice over the mussels and cover the pot tightly.

Steam, tightly covered, for 15–20 minutes, lifting off the lid just to toss the mussels occasionally for even steaming. The mussels will gently and gradually open, and once opened, let them steam another few minutes so the meat is tender yet firm.

Gremolata (garnish)

Prepare the Gremolata while the mussels are steaming. Lightly toast the pine nuts in a dry skillet over medium heat, tossing and watching carefully until golden brown, 1–2 minutes. Finely zest the orange and lemon. Toss the zests with the parsley and toasted pine nuts in a small bowl.

To serve, place 2 to 3 large ladles of mussels in a soup plate with some sauce for each person. Top with some of the Gremolata. Serve with the traditional accompaniment of French fries, the rest of the bottle of white wine, and fresh bread and butter. And make sure that there is a large empty bowl in the middle of the table for the empty shells. And plenty of napkins.

NOTE: There are two ways to eat steamed mussels. One way is to slurp directly from the shell after having scooped up a bit of the sauce. The other is to use one empty shell as a "pincher" to pinch and pull the mussel meat out of the other shells, like a primitive eating utensil.

Pasta with Orange and Speck

2 ounces (60 g) speck, prosciutto, coppa, or other thinly sliced dry-cured ham

2 tablespoons olive oil

1 medium yellow onion, chopped

1 orange, zested and juiced for $1/3$ cup (85 ml)

$3/4$ cup (190 ml) heavy cream

$1/8$ teaspoon salt

Pinch of freshly ground black pepper

$1/4$ teaspoon lemon juice

$10\,1/2$ ounces (300 g) egg fettuccine or tagliatelle, preferably fresh

1 teaspoon chopped fresh oregano or thyme leaves

Freshly grated Parmesan cheese, for serving, optional

ORANGE AND SPECK, A SMOKY DRY-CURED HAM, is an unusual combination of sweet and salty, but one that makes a phenomenal pasta sauce. The orange cream sauce is quick and easy to put together, although you must watch it carefully and stir it often. Then simply toss in fresh pasta with more speck and fresh herbs and you have a flavorful and exceptional dish.

Chop $1/3$ of the speck and shred the rest into thin strips and set aside.

Heat the oil in a large saucepan over medium to medium-high heat and add the onion. Cook, stirring occasionally, until softened, transparent, and beginning to color around the edges, about 5 minutes. Add the chopped speck and cook, stirring, for 2 minutes. Lower the heat only slightly and add the orange juice and about a teaspoon of the zest; cook, stirring, to reduce, 2 minutes.

Add the cream, remaining zest, salt, and pepper. Add the lemon juice and cook, stirring, at a simmer for another 2–3 minutes to reduce and thicken slightly. Taste, and add more salt, pepper, or lemon juice if needed. Remove from the heat.

Bring a large pot of lightly salted water to a boil. Add the pasta and cook, stirring occasionally to keep from clumping, for about 3 minutes for fresh pasta, and according to package instructions for dried. Drain and return the pasta to the pot or to a large serving bowl or platter. Pour the orange cream sauce over the pasta and toss to evenly coat. Add the shredded speck and oregano; stir to mix in. Serve hot with Parmesan cheese on the side for those who desire to add it.

Breads
(Quick and Yeast)

Makes 1 large 10 x 14-inch
(25 x 35 cm) or larger
rectangle

1 1/2 tablespoons granulated
    white sugar

2 1/2 teaspoons (1/4 ounce / 7 g)
    active dry yeast

1 1/4 cups (315 ml) warm water,
    divided

4 cups (19 ounces / 540 g)
    all-purpose flour, divided, plus
    more for kneading

2 teaspoons salt

3 oranges, finely zested, about
    1 1/2 tablespoons

4 tablespoons olive oil, divided

1 to 2 oranges

1 to 1 1/2 yellow or red onions

1 cup (100 g) cured black, green,
    or purple olives

Sea salt flakes, preferably
    smoked, coarse salt, or Orange
    Salt (page 22)

Freshly ground black pepper,
    to taste

Fresh oregano or thyme leaves,
    optional

Savory Orange, Onion, and Olive Focaccia

WHETHER BAKED UP THICK AND FLUFFY or rolled out thin and crispy, this focaccia highlights the delicious combination of onion, orange, and olives, making a fantastic, unusual bread for dinner, a snack, or as part of a light meal. The amount of topping you use will depend on the size of your focaccia as well as the size of your oranges and onions; just know that the flavors mellow and the onions shrink when baked. The focaccia is best eaten warm from the oven but is excellent eaten when cooled.

Place the sugar, yeast, and 1/4 cup (65 ml) of the water in a bowl, and let stand for 15 minutes until the yeast has dissolved and the mixture is foamy.

Place 3 3/4 cups (500 g) of the flour, salt, and zest in a large mixing bowl and rub together with your fingers until blended and there are no clumps of zest; make a well in the center of the flour. Pour 2 tablespoons oil, the yeast mixture, and remaining water into the well and stir with a wooden spoon until a rough dough forms; if there are any pockets of flour that won't blend in, add 1–2 tablespoons more warm water at a time, only as needed.

Turn the dough out onto a lightly floured work surface and knead in the remaining 1/4 cup (40 g) flour. Knead the dough for 6 minutes, dusting both the dough and the work surface lightly with more flour to keep the dough from sticking. The dough should be soft, smooth, and elastic.

Oil a large, clean mixing bowl with 1 tablespoon of the oil. Place the ball of dough in the bowl, turning to coat the surface of the dough with oil. Cover the bowl with plastic wrap and a kitchen towel and let rise for 1 hour until double in size.

Prepare the toppings by peeling the oranges, cutting away all the white pith, and slicing across the core into 1/4-inch (1/2 cm) slices, about 6 slices per orange. If you prefer, slice each round into 4 triangles. Peel and trim the onion and slice as thinly as possible—cut the onion in half if easier—separating the slices into rings.

(continued)

Preheat oven to 400 degrees F (200 degrees C).

Scrape the risen dough onto a lightly floured work surface and roll out into a 10 x 14-inch (25 x 35 cm) rectangle. Transfer to a parchment-lined baking sheet and roll and press back into shape. If you like, use wet fingertips to make indentations across the surface of the dough where a little oil can pool. Brush dough with remaining 1 tablespoon oil and arrange the oranges on the surface; pressing gently into the dough. Spread the onions evenly over the focaccia. Dot with the olives, pressing firmly into the dough, and dust with salt, pepper, and oregano. Bake for 30–40 minutes until risen and golden.

Traditional Cranberry and Orange Walnut Bread

Makes 1 loaf

STREUSEL TOPPING

3 tablespoons all-purpose flour

3 tablespoons light or dark brown sugar

1/4 teaspoon ground cinnamon

2 tablespoons (1 ounce / 30 g) unsalted butter, cubed

BREAD

1 orange, juiced and zested

Boiling water

2 tablespoons (1 ounce / 30 g) unsalted butter, cubed, at room temperature

1 large egg

1 cup granulated white sugar

1 cup (6 1/2 ounces / 200 g) whole or coarsely chopped fresh or frozen (thawed) cranberries

1/2 cup (2 ounces / 50 g) coarsely chopped walnuts or pecans

2 cups (9 1/2 ounces / 270 g) all-purpose flour

1 teaspoon baking powder

1/2 teaspoon baking soda

1/2 teaspoon salt

I FIND CRANBERRIES SO QUINTESSENTIALLY Christmassy, with their bright ruby-red glow and their tangy snap, that as soon as the season rolls around, my kitchen counter is always laden with muffins, breads, coffee cakes, and fruit tarts studded with this most festive of berries. This recipe is a must for your holiday table. Add the streusel topping for a sweeter treat.

Streusel Topping

Place the flour, brown sugar, and cinnamon in a bowl and toss to combine. Add the butter and, using only your fingertips, rub quickly into the dry ingredients until it resembles damp sand and there are no chunks of butter left. Chill in the refrigerator while you prepare the quick bread.

Bread

Preheat oven to 325 degrees F (165 degrees C). Butter a standard 9 x 5 x 2 1/2-inch (23 x 13 x 6 cm) or 8 cup (2 l) loaf pan.

Add enough boiling water to the orange juice to make 3/4 cup (175 ml) of liquid. Add the zest and butter and stir until the butter is melted.

In a large mixing bowl, whisk or beat together the egg and sugar until blended, and light and fluffy. Pour the orange mixture into the egg mixture and stir together. Fold in the cranberries and walnuts.

In a separate bowl, blend together the flour, baking powder, baking soda, and salt. Stir the flour mixture into the orange mixture until well-blended.

Spread the batter into the prepared loaf pan. Sprinkle the streusel evenly over the top of the batter, breaking up any lumps with your fingertips. Bake for 55–60 minutes, or until the center is set and the top is golden brown. Allow to cool in the pan on a rack before sliding a knife around the edges to loosen and unmolding.

Orange, Date, and Pecan Muffins

Makes 12 muffins

1 cup (4.8 ounces / 135 g)
    white whole-wheat or
    all-purpose flour

1/2 cup (1.8 ounces / 50 g)
    chestnut flour (see note)

2 teaspoons baking powder

1/2 teaspoon salt

1/2 teaspoon ground cinnamon

1/2 cup (2 ounces / 55 g) toasted
    wheat germ or oat flakes
    (2 ounces / 57 g)

1/2 cup (2 ounces / 55 g) finely
    chopped pecans

1 to 2 juice oranges

2 large eggs

1/4 cup (65 ml) honey

1/4 cup (65 ml) maple syrup

1/2 cup (125 ml) whole or
    low-fat milk

4 tablespoons (2 ounces / 60 g)
    unsalted butter, melted and
    cooled

1/2 cup (2 1/2 ounces / 75 g)
    coarsely chopped pitted dates

ORANGE, DATE, AND PECAN MUFFINS ARE PROPER breakfast muffins (not too sweet) perfectly cakey while remaining light, tender, and delicately flavored—the orange, date, and cinnamon beautifully balanced. The pecans and the dates, if not overly puréed, add a wonderful toothsome bite. Serve these muffins warm with Honey-Orange Spiced Butter (page 112) for an extra-special treat.

Preheat oven to 375 degrees F (190 degrees C). Generously butter a standard 12-cup muffin tin.

In a large mixing bowl, sift together the flours, baking powder, salt, and cinnamon. Stir in the wheat germ and pecans. Set aside.

Squeeze the oranges for 1/2 cup (125 ml) juice. Coarsely chop half of 1 of the squeezed oranges, pulp, and peel. Place the chopped pulp and peel in a blender with the juice and whiz for about 30 seconds until the peel is finely ground and the mixture is liquid. Add the eggs, honey, maple syrup, milk, butter, and dates. Blend for about 1 minute until the mixture is smooth, or a bit longer if you want the dates completely puréed.

Pour the liquid into the dry ingredients and stir to combine, just until all the dry ingredients are moistened and the batter is well-blended and smooth. Do not overmix.

Pour or spoon the batter into the prepared muffin tin and bake for 20–25 minutes, or until the muffins are risen, set, a deep golden brown, and are just beginning to pull away from the sides of the muffin tin.

NOTE: Chestnut flour adds a delicate but distinctive, slightly nutty, and sweet flavor to these muffins. You can replace it with the same quantity all-purpose flour, but it is worth the effort finding chestnut flour.

Orange Cardamom Scones with Honey-Orange Spiced Butter

Makes 12 scones

3 cups (14 1/2 ounces / 405 g)
  cake flour

1/4 cup (scant 3/4 ounce / 20 g)
  powdered milk or buttermilk

2 teaspoons baking powder

1/2 teaspoon baking soda

1/2 teaspoon salt

1/2 teaspoon ground cardamom

1/2 cup (100 g) granulated white
  sugar

1 large orange, zested

8 tablespoons (4 ounces / 120 g)
  cold butter, cubed

1 large egg

1/2 cup (125 ml) whole milk

4 tablespoons orange juice

1 teaspoon vanilla extract

1/2 teaspoon Orange Extract
  (page 22)

1 egg white

2 tablespoons Orange Sugar
  (page 21), granulated white
  sugar, or granulated light
  brown sugar

(continued)

THIS RECIPE IS A MELDING of my favorite drop scone recipe and a recipe I love from King Arthur Flour for traditional scones. These scones are light and delicate and perfectly cakey with a hint of orange and cardamom and a satisfying sugary crust. Paired, of course, warm from the oven with Honey-Orange Spiced Butter, delicate Orange Cardamom Scones make a pleasurable and special breakfast or teatime snack. Make sure that you blend and knead the dough with a very light hand to ensure a light and delicate crumb.

Preheat oven to 375 degrees F (190 degrees C). Line a large baking sheet with parchment paper.

Combine the flour, powdered milk, baking powder, baking soda, salt, cardamom, sugar, and the zest in a large mixing bowl and whisk to combine, breaking up any clumps of zest. Toss the butter cubes in the dry ingredients to coat and then, using the tips of your fingers, rub quickly into the dry ingredients until it resembles damp sand and there are no chunks of butter left.

In a separate bowl, whisk together the egg, milk, juice, and vanilla and orange extracts until combined. Pour over the dry ingredients and stir lightly with a fork just until combined and all of the dry ingredients are moistened and a dough has formed. Do not overmix.

Turn the dough out onto a lightly floured surface and quickly, very lightly, and gently fold and knead just until the dough is smooth and homogeneous and is no longer sticky, only 30 seconds to 1 minute. Cut the dough into 2 equal portions and shape each into a thick, round disc. Place each disc on the prepared baking sheet, lightly dust with flour, and gently roll into an even 1/2-inch-thick (1 cm), 7-inch (18 cm) round circle.

(continued)

HONEY-ORANGE SPICED
BUTTER

8 tablespoons (4 ounces / 120 g)
   unsalted butter, softened to
   room temperature

1 teaspoon honey

1 tablespoon orange juice

1 teaspoon very fine orange zest

1/8 teaspoon ground cinnamon

Pinch of ground cardamom

Pinch of ground nutmeg

Using a sharp knife, slice each circle into 8 even wedges, gently separating the pieces. Dipping the knife in flour between cuts makes this easier, keeping the dough from sticking to the knife. Brush each scone with egg white and dust generously with sugar.

Bake for about 25 minutes, or until well risen and a golden brown and a sugary crust has formed. Serve warm with Honey-Orange Spiced Butter.

Honey-Orange Spiced Butter

Add butter, honey, juice, zest, cinnamon, cardamom, and nutmeg to a small mixing bowl and beat until well-combined, light, and fluffy. Allow to firm slightly in the refrigerator before serving with the warm scones.

Sweet Potato Biscuits

1 large or 2 small sweet potatoes,
about 1 pound (500 g)

Olive oil

1 orange, finely zested

1/2 cup (125 ml) orange juice

1 tablespoon minced fresh
sage leaves

Freshly ground black pepper,
to taste

1/4 cup (65 ml) whole milk
or buttermilk

3 to 3 1/2 cups (405 to 475 g)
all-purpose flour

2 tablespoons packed or
granulated light brown sugar

4 teaspoons baking powder

1/4 teaspoon baking soda

1 teaspoon salt

6 tablespoons (3 ounces / 90 g)
unsalted butter, chilled
and cubed

1 tablespoon (1/2 ounce / 15 g)
melted salted butter

THESE FLAKY, LIGHT, AND TENDER BISCUITS are delicately flavored with sweet potatoes, orange, and sage, and are perfect served for a family dinner or a holiday meal, breakfast, or brunch. Brushing the potato wedges with a bit of olive oil keeps them from crisping around the edges, but they can be baked without the oil. You can bake the biscuits as soon as you prepare the dough, but chilling it makes the biscuits even more tender and flavorful.

Preheat oven to 400 degrees F (200 degrees C). Wash and dry the sweet potatoes, trim off the ends, and slice lengthwise into 8 wedges. Place the wedges on an aluminum foil–lined baking sheet, brush very lightly with oil, and bake for about 15 minutes until very fork tender.

Remove the potatoes from the oven and allow to cool until easy to handle. Scrape the soft potato from the skins into a large bowl and mash for 3/4 cups (185 to 190 ml) smooth purée. Whisk in the zest, juice, sage, pepper, and milk.

In a separate bowl, stir together 3 cups (405 g) flour, brown sugar, baking powder, baking soda, and salt. Toss in the cubed butter to coat then, using thumb and fingertips, rub into the dry ingredients until it resembles coarse meal or sand with no large lumps of butter left; small bits and even pea-size lumps of butter add flakiness to the biscuits.

Fold the dry ingredients, 1/3 at a time, into the purée until a manageable dough, soft but no longer sticky, forms. Fold or knead in more flour if needed. Turn the dough out onto a floured work surface and knead briefly and lightly, just until the dough is smooth and firm enough to roll and cut. Wrap the dough in plastic wrap and refrigerate to chill, a few hours to overnight.

Preheat oven to 425 degrees F (220 degrees C). Remove the dough from the refrigerator; it should be firm but still soft and pliable, lightly roll out the dough—not too much pressure from the rolling pin—to an even thickness of 1 inch (2 cm). Using a 2 1/2-inch (6 cm) biscuit cutter, cut out biscuit rounds and place on an ungreased baking sheet. Gather up the scraps, knead together lightly, roll out, and cut more biscuits until all the dough has been used.

Bake for 15 minutes or until the biscuits are puffed up, the sides cracked and layered, and are lightly colored. Remove from the oven and immediately brush the tops with melted butter. Serve the biscuits hot or warm.

Glazed Apple and Orange Braid

Makes a 14-inch (36 cm)
coffee cake

DOUGH

- 2 tablespoons warm water
- 2 1/2 teaspoons (1/4 ounce / 7 g) active dry yeast
- 1/2 cup (125 ml) milk
- 6 tablespoons (50 g) granulated white sugar
- 5 tablespoons (2 1/2 ounces / 75 g) unsalted butter, softened to room temperature
- 1 teaspoon salt
- 2 large egg yolks
- 1 large orange, finely zested and juiced, juice reserved for glaze
- 1/2 teaspoon ground cardamom
- 1/2 teaspoon ground nutmeg
- 2 to 2 1/2 cups (9 1/2 to 12 ounces / 270 to 335 g) all-purpose flour, divided

AUTUMN IS APPLE SEASON, AND I FIND MYSELF BAKING with many varieties all season long—cakes, puddings, pies, and even spiced baked apples. This warm, glazed coffee cake laden with apples will surprise with the gentle tang and sweetness of orange, and is definitely my favorite coffee cake. A masterful hint of cardamom and nutmeg, and a homey scent of cinnamon make this a truly comforting treat on a chilly fall day.

This is a wonderful recipe given to me by a friend many years ago that I have since put my own spin on. The dough is surprisingly easy to make, soft and silky to handle, and when baked, rises light and tender. The filling is made in a flash using firm pie apples that are able to hold their shape after baking. The orange glaze is the perfect finishing touch.

Dough

Place the water and yeast in a small cup and let stand until the yeast dissolves and is frothy, about 6 minutes.

Put the milk, sugar, butter, and salt in a small saucepan and heat gently over medium-low heat until the sugar dissolves and the butter melts. The mixture should be just warm. Pour this into a large mixing bowl. Whisk in the yeast mixture, egg yolks, 1 teaspoon zest, cardamom, and nutmeg. Fold in 2 cups (270 g) of the flour until a dough comes together. Turn the dough out onto a well-floured surface and knead gently, adding extra flour, 1 tablespoon at a time, until the dough is smooth and silky.

Place the dough into a large clean bowl. Cover with plastic wrap, placing it against the surface of the dough to keep it from forming a crust, and then cover with a kitchen towel. Place in a warm, draft-free area and allow to rise for 2–2 1/2 hours, until double in size.

2 tablespoons (1 ounce / 30 g)
  unsalted butter

6 tablespoons (50 g) dark or light
  brown sugar

5 medium pie apples, peeled,
  cored and sliced

1 teaspoon finely grated
  orange zest

1 teaspoon finely grated
  lemon zest

1/2 teaspoon ground cinnamon

1/8 teaspoon ground cardamom

1/8 teaspoon ground nutmeg

GLAZE

1 cup (4 1/2 ounces / 125 g)
  confectioners' sugar

1 1/2 to 2 tablespoons reserved
  orange juice, divided

Filling

Melt the butter in a large, heavy skillet over medium-high heat. Add the brown sugar and cook, stirring, until you have a thick, grainy sauce, about 1 minute. Add the apple slices, tossing to coat completely with the sauce, and cook until the apples are tender and the sauce has been reduced to a glaze, about 7 minutes. Mix in the zests and the spices and toss apples to evenly coat. Cool the filling at least 30 minutes, or up to 3 hours, before assembling the braid.

Assembling the Braid

Roll the dough out onto a well-floured surface into a 12 x 14-inch (30 x 36 cm) rectangle. Slide the dough onto a large length of parchment paper, and using your rolling pin, straighten the dough back into an even rectangle if necessary. Arrange the apple mixture down the center of the dough, leaving a 1-inch (2 1/2 cm) border of dough at the top and bottom shorter ends and 3–4 inches (8–10 cm) on each side. Starting about 1 inch (2 cm) from the apples, slice straight out to the edge of the dough with a sharp knife at 1-inch (2 cm) intervals, making about 13 strips down each side; feel free to use a tape measure. Starting at the top, fold the strips of dough over the filling on a slight angle, overlapping the strips, to form a lattice down the center. Seal the open ends of the dough at the top and bottom.

Carefully slide the parchment paper onto a large baking sheet. Cover loosely with plastic wrap and a dishtowel and let rise for 1–1 1/2 hours; the dough will have puffed but will not be double in size.

Preheat oven to 375 degrees F (190 degrees C). Bake, uncovered, for 30–35 minutes, until golden brown. Carefully slide a spatula underneath and lift up just to make sure that the underside is also golden brown. Remove from the oven and slide the parchment and braid onto a cooling rack. Cool for 30 minutes. Drizzle the orange glaze over top before serving.

Glaze

In a small bowl, stir the confectioners' sugar and 1 1/2 tablespoons juice together until well-blended and a thick glaze forms, adding a bit more juice if too thick, a bit more sugar if too thin.

NOTE: Choose a pie apple for this recipe, a flavorful, sweet-tart variety that bakes tender and juicy while holding its shape, such as Braeburn or Jonagold.

Stacy's Orange and Rosemary Boule

Makes 1 loaf

2 1/2 to 3 cups (12 to 14 ounces / 335 to 400 g) unbleached white whole-wheat flour, divided

2 teaspoons (1/4 ounce / 7 g) active dry yeast

1/2 cup (125 ml) warm water, divided

1 rounded tablespoon finely minced fresh rosemary leaves

1/2 cup (125 ml) orange juice, at room temperature

2 tablespoons grated orange zest, plus more for garnish

2 tablespoons olive oil, plus more

2 tablespoons honey

1 teaspoon sea salt

2 tablespoons milk

Fresh rosemary sprigs, for garnish

MY FRIEND STACY LIVINGSTON RUSHTON LIVES the expat life like I do. But whereas I've spent the last 30 years between France and Italy, Stacy has lived in almost 15 countries spread out over 6 of the 7 continents. A great home cook such as Stacy can't help but be influenced by the cuisines of the different cultures and countries she has lived in and been a part of, recipes—and stories—that she shares on her blog, foodlustpeoplelove.com.

Her Orange and Rosemary Boule, a traditional French round country loaf, is a gorgeous, flawless, flavorful bread just this side of a brioche, inspired by the marvelous, crusty-on-the-outside, tender-on-the-inside artisan breads she ate while living in Paris. Rosemary is a much-used herb in France for both savory and sweet foods. At the hotel, I flavor strawberry and peach jams with rosemary, and it goes exquisitely with orange.

Measure 1 cup (5 ounces / 135 g) of flour into a large mixing bowl and make a well in the center. Sprinkle the yeast into the well, and then pour in 1/4 cup (65 ml) warm water. Allow the yeast to activate for 15 minutes. Once the yeast is foamy, add the remaining water, rosemary, juice, zest, oil, honey, and salt to the flour mixture and combine until well-blended. Stir in the remaining flour, 1/2 cup (65 g) at a time, until you have a soft dough just firm enough to begin kneading by hand.

Sprinkle some of the remaining flour on your work surface and turn the dough out of the bowl. Knead for 5–6 minutes, flouring the work surface and the dough with the remaining flour as needed until you have a smooth, elastic dough that is no longer sticky. Oil the mixing bowl, shape the dough into a ball, and place the ball into the bowl, rolling to coat the dough completely with the oil. Cover the bowl with plastic wrap, then with a clean kitchen towel, and put in a warm place for about 1 hour to rise until double in size.

(continued)

When double in size, punch down the dough, turn it out onto a floured work surface, and knead again for 1–2 minutes. Lightly grease a 9- or 10-inch (22 to 25 cm) round baking pan. Form the dough into a smooth ball and place it in the greased pan. Cover it with the mixing bowl and put it in a warm place for a second rising, about 1 hour.

Preheat oven to 350 degrees F (180 degrees C).

Using a very sharp knife cut a cross in the top of the dough just deep enough that it holds the mark. Gently brush milk all over the top of the boule with a pastry brush. Sprinkle the top with extra zest and press sprigs of rosemary into the dough.

Bake for 40–45 minutes; the crust should be a deep golden brown and the loaf should sound hollow when tapped. Remove from the oven and allow to cool slightly before transferring it from the pan onto a cooling rack to cool before slicing.

NOTE: The unbleached whole-wheat flour can be replaced with an equal amount of regular all-purpose flour, adding more as needed for a smooth dough.

Christmas Stollen Wreath

1 cup (6 ounces / 170 g) firmly
  packed dried cranberries

3 tablespoons orange juice

1 tablespoon Grand Marnier or
  Cointreau

1/4 cup (65 ml) lukewarm water

4 1/2 teaspoons (1/2 ounce / 14 g)
  active dry yeast

1 cup (250 ml) milk

10 tablespoons (5 ounces / 150 g)
  unsalted butter, cubed

3 large eggs

2 teaspoons vanilla extract

5 1/2 cups (27 ounces / 770 g)
  all-purpose flour, plus more as
  needed

1/2 cup (100 g) granulated white
  sugar

1 tablespoon Orange Sugar (page
  21) or granulated white
  sugar

3 tablespoons finely ground
  almonds

1 cup (3 1/2 ounces / 100 g)
  slivered almonds

3/4 teaspoon salt

1 teaspoon ground cinnamon

Finely grated zest of 1 lemon

Finely grated zest of 1 orange

3/4 cup (5 ounces / 135 g)
  chopped candied orange peel

(continued)

WHEN IT COMES TO CELEBRATING ANY HOLIDAY I am always in charge of the food, and I find no greater joy than discovering new dishes and pastries that have long, deep traditions. This yeast version of a traditional German Christmas stollen immediately became a family favorite, even if it takes a bit of time to prepare. I recommend using a tape measure when cutting the dough circle in order to guarantee that the slices are equally spaced and the segments are even. Stollen is wonderful for breakfast, snacktime, or dessert.

Prepare the dough the day before baking.

Soak the cranberries in the orange juice and Grand Marnier in a small bowl while you prepare the dough.

Pour the water and yeast into a small bowl, and let stand 5 minutes. Stir to dissolve yeast completely. In a small saucepan, warm the milk and butter over medium-low heat just until the butter has melted. Remove from heat and let stand until lukewarm, about 5 minutes. Lightly beat the eggs in a small bowl and add the vanilla.

In a large mixing bowl, stir together the flour, sugar, Orange Sugar, ground and slivered almonds, salt, cinnamon, and zests. Stir in the dissolved yeast, eggs, milk mixture, cranberries with soaking liquid, and orange peel, adding up to an additional 1/2 cup (65 g) or so flour to the dough if needed in order to have a working consistency. This should take about 2 minutes. You should have a soft, slightly sticky dough. Cover the bowl with plastic wrap or a clean kitchen towel and let rest for 10 minutes.

Scrape the dough out onto a well-floured work surface and knead for 8 minutes until you have a soft and satiny smooth bread dough consistency, flouring the dough and work surface as needed. It may be slightly tacky, but not sticky, and the dried fruit and nuts should be evenly distributed.

Transfer the dough to a lightly oiled bowl, rolling it around to coat with the oil. Cover the bowl with plastic wrap and store in the refrigerator overnight. Because of the butter content, the dough will become very firm in the refrigerator but it will rise slowly. The raw dough can be kept in the refrigerator for up to a week and then baked on the day you want.

(continued)

4 to 6 tablespoons cinnamon
  sugar

2 tablespoons (30 g) melted
  unsalted butter

Confectioners' sugar

Marzipan, sugared cranberries,
  and candied orange peel for
  decoration, if desired

When ready to bake, remove dough from the refrigerator and allow to rest at room temperature for 2 hours. Line a large baking sheet with parchment paper.

Once the dough has rested, scrape it out onto a floured work surface, punch it down, and roll out into a 16 x 24-inch (40 x 60 cm) rectangle about 1/4-inch (1 cm) thick. Sprinkle the dough generously with cinnamon sugar all the way to the edges. Starting with a long side, roll the dough up tightly, forming a long, thin cylinder and transfer to the prepared baking sheet. Pull the ends around together, forming the dough into a ring and join the ends, overlapping the layers to make the seam stronger; pinch to seal.

Using clean kitchen scissors, make cuts along the outside of the circle at 2-inch (5 cm) intervals, cutting 2/3 of the way through the dough. Once sliced, gently pull the sections out from each other so they will stay separated once risen and baked. Tap the wreath lightly with a vegetable oil–soaked paper towel. Cover loosely yet completely with plastic wrap then a clean kitchen towel and allow to rise at room temperature for 2 hours until at least 1 1/2 times the original size.

Preheat oven to 350 degrees F (180 degrees C).

Bake the stollen for 20 minutes then rotate the pan 180 degrees for even baking and continue to bake for 20–30 minutes until the bread is a deep, dark golden caramel color and sounds hollow when thumped on the bottom.

Transfer to a cooling rack and immediately brush the top with melted butter while still hot then sprinkle a generous layer of confectioners' sugar over the top through a sieve or sifter. Wait for 1 minute then tap another layer of sugar over the first. The bread should be coated thickly with the sugar. Let cool at least 1 hour before serving.

To decorate for the holidays, cut out holly leaf shapes from the marzipan that has been tinted green, dip several whole cranberries in egg white then toss to coat completely in granulated white sugar, and place, along with several candied orange peels, on top and around the base of the wreath.

Cookies and Treats

Navette Cookies from Marseille

Makes 12 cookies

1/2 cup (100 g) granulated white sugar

1 large egg

1 rounded teaspoon orange zest

3 teaspoons orange blossom water

3 tablespoons olive oil

1/4 teaspoon salt

1 3/4 cups plus 2 tablespoons (9 ounces / 250 g) all-purpose flour

Milk, for brushing the cookies before baking

IT ISN'T OFTEN THAT WE FIND TRADITIONAL FRENCH pastries flavored with orange, but these wonderful cookies from the Mediterranean port city of Marseille are fragrant with orange blossom water and orange zest. Tender on the inside with the barest crunch on the outside when warm, *navettes* become crispier as they cool, all the better to dunk them in a mug of coffee or tea, or a glass of milk. Navettes are shaped like the little boats they are named after, and are traditionally eaten in Marseilles for the February holiday of Candlemas—*le Chandeleur*—while the rest of the country celebrates with crêpes. We love these olive oil and orange blossom water pastries all year round.

In a medium mixing bowl, beat the sugar and the egg on medium-high speed until pale, thick, and creamy, about 2 minutes. Beat in the zest, orange blossom water, and oil.

Stir the salt into the flour and then beat 2/3 of the flour into the batter in 2 or 3 additions. Finish folding the flour in by hand, kneading until all of the flour has been added and a smooth dough has developed. Form the dough into a ball, wrap in plastic wrap, and refrigerate for 1 hour.

Preheat oven to 350 degrees F (180 degrees C). Line a baking sheet with parchment paper.

Take the dough out of the refrigerator and slightly flatten the ball into a disc. Cut the dough into 12 even wedges. Roll each wedge into a 3-inch-long (7 cm) oval log and place on the prepared baking sheet. Shape the pieces of dough into small "navettes" or little boats by pressing to flatten just a bit, and pinching the 2 ends into rounded points. Make a 2-inch (5 cm) slit down the center of each with a sharp knife, cutting only halfway down into the dough, and carefully push the slit open slightly. Brush each cookie lightly with milk.

Bake for 20–25 minutes, or until golden; the tips and undersides should be a deeper golden brown. Remove from the oven and allow the cookies to cool on a rack. Store in a covered container.

Orange-Glazed
Orange Cream Puffs

CREAM PUFFS (CHOUX)

1 cup (250 ml) water

8 tablespoons (4 ounces / 120 g)
   unsalted butter

1/4 teaspoon salt

1 cup (5 ounces / 135 g)
   all-purpose flour

4 large eggs

THESE CREAM PUFFS ARE REMINISCENT of the pudding-filled choux pastries (cream puffs) that my dad made us throughout my childhood—they were a favorite treat. I gave this delicate French confection a Florida twist by filling the cream puffs with silky orange pastry cream and topping them with an intensely orange glaze. Both the cream puffs and pastry cream can be made the day before assembling; store the puffs in an airtight container and the pastry cream in the refrigerator overnight.

Cream Puffs (Choux)

Preheat oven to 375 degrees F (190 degrees C). Lightly grease a large baking sheet or line with parchment paper.

Heat the water, butter, and salt in a large saucepan over medium heat until the butter melts and the mixture comes to a boil. Add the flour all at once, and using a wooden spoon, stir vigorously until the mixture forms a ball and pulls away from the sides of the pan, 2–3 minutes. Remove from heat and allow to cool for a few minutes. Scraping the dough into a heatproof mixing bowl will speed up the cooling process.

Add the eggs, 1 at a time, stirring vigorously after each addition until blended in.

Using a tablespoon (or teaspoon for smaller puffs), scoop up mounds of dough and carefully push dough off onto the prepared baking sheet. During baking, they will rise and almost double in size, so leave plenty of space between the puffs.

Bake for 30–35 minutes until puffed and lightly golden. Working quickly, open the oven, and with a sharp knife, make a small slit in the side of each puff to allow steam to escape. Bake for an additional 5–10 minutes, depending upon the size of the puffs, until golden brown. Remove from the oven and allow to cool completely before filling with Orange Pastry Cream.

$^1/4$ cup (1 ounce / 30 g)
  cornstarch

2 cups (500 ml) whole milk,
  divided

$^1/2$ cup (100 g) granulated white
  sugar

4 large egg yolks

2 teaspoons freshly grated
  orange zest

3 to 4 tablespoons orange juice

$^1/2$ teaspoon orange blossom
  water or Orange Extract (page
  22), optional

4 tablespoons (2 ounces / 60 g)
  unsalted butter, at room
  temperature

2 tablespoons orange juice,
  divided, plus more as needed

1 cup (4 ounces / 115 g)
  confectioners' sugar, plus more
  as needed

$^1/8$ teaspoon orange blossom
  water or Orange Extract
  (page 22), optional

Orange Pastry Cream

In a large heatproof bowl, dissolve the cornstarch in $^1/2$ cup (125 ml) milk; whisk until smooth.

In a medium saucepan, combine the remaining milk with the sugar. Bring to a boil, and immediately remove from heat.

Beat the egg yolks into the cornstarch mixture, and then pour the scalded milk into the egg mixture in a very slow stream, whisking constantly so the eggs do not cook or curdle. Once all of the hot milk has been whisked into the egg mixture, pour it back into the saucepan and return to the heat. Add the zest, juice, and orange blossom water or extract, if using. Cook over low heat, whisking until the cream thickens and comes just to a boil, 3–5 minutes, no longer. Remove from heat and whisk in the butter until melted.

Pour the cream into a heatproof glass or stainless steel bowl. Press plastic wrap firmly against the surface and refrigerate until chilled.

Use the pastry cream while it is creamy enough to pipe into the cream puffs. If it becomes too firm, beat with an electric mixer on low until creamy and of piping consistency.

To fill the cream puffs, make a hole in the bottom of each puff with a small paring knife. Fit a pastry bag with a $^1/4$-inch ($^1/2$ cm or slightly larger) plain round tip. Fill the bag with the pastry cream then fill each puff by inserting the tip through the opening and squeezing the cream inside. Alternately, use a serrated knife to split cream puffs in half horizontally, spoon the pastry cream onto the bottom halves, and replace the tops.

Orange Glaze

In a small bowl, slowly add 1 $^1/2$ tablespoons orange juice to the confectioners' sugar, stirring to make a smooth, pourable glaze. If too thick to drizzle, add a bit more orange juice. If too thin, stir in more sugar. Adding a few drops of Orange Extract will reinforce the orange flavor; adding a few drops of orange blossom water will add a complexity and warmth to the delicate flavor. Drizzle over the cream puffs or dunk the tops into the bowl of glaze.

Chocolate Orange Grand Marnier Marbled Madeleines

Makes 12 (3-inch / 7 1/2 cm), or 20 (1 1/2-inch / 4 cm) Madeleines

2 large eggs

10 tablespoons (5 ounces / 150 g) unsalted butter, at room temperature, plus more for the molds

1/2 cup plus 2 tablespoons and 2 teaspoons (5 ounces / 140 g) granulated white sugar

1/2 medium orange, finely zested and juiced

2 tablespoons Grand Marnier

Pinch of salt

Scant 3/4 cup (3 1/2 ounces / 100 g) all-purpose flour

1 packed tablespoon (9 g) unsweetened cocoa powder

1/2 teaspoon vanilla extract

WHO CAN RESIST A TENDER, DELICATE, MOIST, AND BUTTERY Madeleine, the traditional little French teacake? These are flavorful with orange, Grand Marnier, and chocolate; the light and dark batters marbled for a beautiful effect. Double the recipe if a dozen isn't enough. Don't expect huge, classic humps in the center of each Madeleine, the cakes will only puff up slightly.

Preheat oven to 400 degrees F (200 degrees C). Lightly butter a 12 x 3-inch (30 x 7.5 cm) Madeleine mold.

Separate the eggs, placing the whites with a few grains of salt in a very clean bowl, preferably plastic or metal. Set aside.

In a large mixing bowl, beat the butter and sugar together until well-blended and fluffy. Beat in the egg yolks, zest, juice, Grand Marnier, and salt until smooth. Scrape down the sides of the bowl, add the flour, and beat just until combined and smooth.

Using very clean beaters, whip the egg whites to firm but not stiff peaks. Fold the whipped egg whites into the batter until completely blended in and no white is visible. The batter should be thick and very smooth.

Divide the batter evenly into 2 bowls. Using a spatula, fold the cocoa powder and vanilla into 1 of the bowls, until well-blended. Spoon equal parts of each batter into the indentations of the prepared pan, about 3/4 full. Marble the 2 batters together by dragging the tip of a sharp knife through the 2 colors of batter to create a swirl pattern in each Madeleine.

Bake for 15–20 minutes; if making mini Madeleines, the baking time will be closer to 10 minutes. Remove the mold from the oven when the center of each Madeleine is set and puffed and the edges are golden. Allow to cool for 1–2 minutes in the mold before popping them out, one by one, using the point of a sharp knife and a gentle hand, or turning the mold over and tapping on the bottom. Cool completely on a cooling rack.

Hazelnut Orange Icebox Cookies with Two Fillings

Makes about 60 cookies

HAZELNUT ORANGE ICEBOX COOKIES

16 tablespoons (8 ounces / 240 g) butter, at room temperature

1/2 cup (3 1/2 ounces / 100 g) packed light brown sugar

1/2 cup (100 g) granulated white sugar

1 large egg

2 tablespoons orange juice

2 teaspoons finely grated orange zest

1/2 teaspoon finely grated lemon zest

1/4 teaspoon Orange Extract (page 22)

2 3/4 cups (13 ounces / 370 g) all-purpose flour

1/2 teaspoon baking soda

1/2 teaspoon baking powder

1/2 teaspoon salt

3/4 cup (2 1/2 ounces / 75 g) finely chopped hazelnuts

(continued)

HAZELNUT ORANGE ICEBOX COOKIES ARE DELICATE, butter-rich shortbread cookies chilled in the refrigerator overnight to firm the dough before slicing and baking, allowing you to slice off and bake just as many or as few as you like at a time. You can substitute unsalted pistachios, pecans, or walnuts for the hazelnuts, as each of them pair deliciously with orange. Enjoy the cookies plain, or top single or sandwich two cookies together with a dollop of either of the two fillings provided with this recipe. Or spoon the Orange Mascarpone Cream into individual ramekins and serve as a dip for the cookies for a fun dessert.

In a large mixing bowl, beat the butter and sugars together until smooth and creamy. Beat in the egg then add the juice, zests, and extract and beat until combined.

In a separate bowl, stir together the flour, baking soda, baking powder, salt, and nuts. Beat the dry ingredients into the creamed mixture in 3 additions, until well-combined. The dough should be creamy and soft but stiff. Cover the bowl with plastic wrap and chill in the refrigerator for 2 hours.

Once the dough has chilled and stiffened, remove it from the refrigerator and divide into 2 equal portions; work half of the dough at a time, returning the second half back to the refrigerator.

Quickly, but gently, shape the dough into a 10-inch long (3.8 x 25 cm) log, 1 1/2 inches (4 cm) in diameter, rolling the dough on a lightly floured work surface. Once the log is shaped, making sure it is the same diameter end to end, wrap the log in plastic wrap and refrigerate for 24 hours. Repeat with the second half of the dough.

When ready to bake, preheat oven to 350 degrees F (180 degrees C). Lightly grease or line a large baking sheet with parchment paper.

(continued)

ORANGE MASCARPONE CREAM

7 ounces (200 g) mascarpone, drained

1 ounce (30 g) fresh goat cheese or ricotta, drained

2 tablespoons Orange Sugar (page 21) or vanilla sugar

1 teaspoon finely grated orange zest

$1/8$ teaspoon ground cinnamon

2 tablespoons orange juice

$1/2$ to 1 teaspoon Grand Marnier

$1/2$ cup (125 ml) heavy whipping cream

CREAM CHEESE AND GRAND MARNIER FILLING

4 ounces (115 g) cream cheese, slightly softened

4 tablespoons (2 ounces / 60 g) unsalted butter, slightly softened

1 teaspoon Grand Marnier

$1 1/4$ cups (5 $1/2$ ounces / 160 g) confectioners' sugar

Remove 1 of the dough logs from the refrigerator and discard the plastic wrap. Using a very sharp knife, cut the dough into even $1/4$-inch-thick ($1/2$ cm) slices and place on the prepared baking sheet, leaving space in between the cookies so they can spread. Bake for 10 minutes, or until puffed slightly, just set, and a pale golden color. Remove from the oven and leave the cookies to cool for just 2–3 minutes before transferring them to a rack to cool completely. After the cookies have cooled, use your choice of fillings to make sandwich cookies.

Orange Mascarpone Cream

Makes 2 cups (500 ml)

Place the mascaarpone, goat cheese, Orange Sugar, zest, cinnamon, juice, and Grand Marnier in a large mixing bowl and beat until blended and creamy. Place in the refrigerator to chill and firm before using.

Once the cookies have been baked and cooled, beat the whipping cream until very thick. Beat the Orange Mascarpone Cream briefly, just to loosen and smooth. Fold the whipped cream into the Orange Mascarpone Cream and then beat briefly to thicken.

Cream Cheese and Grand Marnier Filling

Makes 1 cup (250 ml)

Beat cream cheese, butter, Grand Marnier, and sugar together until smooth.

French Orange Financiers

5 1/3 tablespoons (2.7 ounces /
75 g) unsalted butter, plus
more for the molds

4 large egg whites

1 cup (3 1/2 ounces / 100 g) finely
ground almonds or hazelnuts

5 tablespoons (2 ounces / 50 g)
all-purpose flour

1/3 cup plus 1 teaspoon
(2 1/2 ounces / 75 g) granulated
white sugar

1/3 cup plus 1 tablespoon (2 1/2
ounces / 75 g) granulated
brown sugar

Pinch of salt

1 tablespoon Orange Powder
(page 19) or finely grated
orange zest

1/4 teaspoon vanilla extract

1/4 teaspoon orange blossom
water or Orange Extract
(page 22)

FINANCIERS ARE TINY, DELICATE FRENCH TEACAKES, a cross between a cookie and a sponge cake. Financiers, unlike their *chère cousine la Madeleine (dear cousin Madeleine)*, are lightened and moistened with plenty of whipped egg whites and are flavored with lots of finely ground nuts. Delicate and tender on the inside with a crisp yet slightly chewy crust, financiers are rather rich and very satisfying, and quite addictive, so try not to eat too many at once.

Preheat oven to 400 degrees F (200 degrees C). Generously butter 16 traditional (approximately 3 3/4 x 1 3/4-inch / 9 1/2 x 4 1/2 cm) rectangular financier molds; you can use any shallow baking molds you have that are of equivalent capacity or volume. This is most easily done with melted and cooled or softened unsalted butter and a pastry brush.

Slowly melt the butter over low heat in a small saucepan and remove from the heat just as the last bit of butter is melting; set aside to cool briefly.

Beat the egg whites in a medium mixing bowl with a few grains of salt until dense and stiff peaks hold. In a large mixing bowl, combine and whisk together the ground almonds, flour, sugars, salt, and Orange Powder or zest.

Gently fold 3 or 4 tablespoons of the dry ingredients into the egg whites, and then fold that egg white mixture into the remaining dry ingredients just until smooth and completely blended; do not over fold.

Gently fold in the butter, a little at a time, slowly pouring the melted butter down the side of the bowl rather than onto the batter. Add the vanilla and orange blossom water with the last addition of the butter. Spoon the batter evenly into the molds, filling each mold no more than 3/4 full.

Bake for 12–15 minutes or until the financiers are puffed, firm to the touch, and evenly golden. Remove from the oven, allow to cool for about 5 minutes in the molds, and then gently pop the financiers out of the molds and cool completely on cooling racks.

VARIATION: For additional flavor options, consider using 3 tablespoons (approximately 2 ounces / 57 g) finely grated semisweet chocolate or 1/4 teaspoon ground cinnamon added to the dry ingredients, or 2 tablespoons fresh or frozen blueberries, 3 per financier, pressed into the batter after it has been poured into the molds.

Chocolate Orange Marmalade Brownies

Makes 1 (9-inch / 23 cm)
square pan of brownies

2 ounces (60 g) unsweetened or bitter baking chocolate

1 ounce (30 g) orange-infused 70 percent dark chocolate, such as Lindt Excellence Orange Intense

3/4 cup (3 1/2 ounces / 105 g) all-purpose flour

1/4 teaspoon baking powder

1/4 teaspoon salt

8 tablespoons (4 ounces / 115 g) unsalted butter, at room temperature

1 cup (6 ounces / 170 g) light or golden brown sugar

1/4 cup (50 g) granulated white sugar

2 large eggs

1/2 teaspoon vanilla extract

1 tablespoon Grand Marnier or Cointreau or 1/2 teaspoon Orange Extract (page 22)

3 heaping tablespoons bitter orange marmalade

THERE MAY BE NOTHING BETTER THAN LUSCIOUS, moist brownies of deep, dark chocolate infused with the kick of Grand Marnier and bitter orange marmalade. These orangey brownies make a homey, comforting snack as well as an intriguing and sophisticated dessert simply topped with a froth of whipped cream or a scoop of ice cream and a drizzle of ganache. The orange-infused chocolate can be replaced by bitter or semisweet chocolate.

Preheat the oven to 350 degrees F (180 degrees C). Lightly butter a 9-inch (23 cm) square pan or line with foil or parchment paper, leaving several inches overhanging 2 opposite sides for lifting the brownies out of the pan; lightly butter the foil or parchment.

Slowly melt both chocolates together in a double boiler over simmering hot water. Remove from the heat when all but a 1/4 of the chocolate has melted then stir vigorously until all the chocolate is melted and smooth. If necessary, place back over the heat until completely melted. Set aside to cool slightly.

Combine the flour, baking powder, and salt in a bowl, whisking to blend.

In a large mixing bowl, beat the butter and sugars together until light, smooth, and creamy. Beat in the eggs, 1 at a time, just until combined. Add the vanilla, Grand Marnier, and melted chocolate and beat until smooth and blended, scraping down the bowl as necessary.

Fold in the dry ingredients by hand until well-blended and smooth. Do not over mix. Gently swirl in the orange marmalade, completely combining for an overall orange flavor, or combine less thoroughly to create small pockets of orange marmalade; scrape the batter into the prepared pan and smooth. Alternately, pour the batter into the prepared pan, spoon the marmalade onto the brownies and swirl in with a knife. Bake for about 30 minutes, until the center is set but still moist.

Remove from the oven and allow to cool on a rack before slicing. If the pan was lined with foil or parchment, allow the brownies to cool for 10 minutes before lifting them out to a cooling rack; this stops the brownies from continuing to bake further in the hot pan.

Orange Pecan Shortbread with Dried Cherries

Makes 1 (8 1/2-inch / 22 cm) round shortbread, 16 slices

1 3/4 cups (8 ounces / 225 g) cake flour, measured then sifted

1/2 cup (100 g) granulated white sugar

1/8 teaspoon salt

2 oranges, zested

8 tablespoons (4 ounces / 115 g) chilled unsalted butter, cubed

1/2 cup (2 ounces / 50 g) finely chopped pecans or walnuts

1/3 cup (2 ounces / 50 g) dried cherries or cranberries, coarsely chopped, blueberries, or mini chocolate chips

2 tablespoons orange juice

THIS SHORTBREAD IS A FRUITY TWIST on a traditional English teatime snack. Classic shortbread is rather plain, but mine is chock-full of nuts and dried fruit. Shortbread is normally dry and crumbly, but this version remains tender enough to please everyone. It's the perfect treat to accompany a cup of tea.

Preheat oven to 350 degrees F (180 degrees C). Line the bottom of an 8 1/2-inch (22 cm) round springform pan with parchment paper. Butter and flour the sides of the pan.

Combine the flour, sugar, salt, and zest in a large mixing bowl and toss to blend. Rub the butter into the flour mixture with your fingertips until it's the texture of damp sand and there are no more lumps of butter. Stir in the pecans and cherries until evenly distributed. Add the juice, and using a fork, toss and stir until the dough starts to bind. Gather up the dough and knead, first in the bowl, until a dough is formed and there are no more pockets of dry ingredients left, then on a lightly-floured work surface, working lightly and quickly until the dough is smooth. Push and flatten the dough into a rough disc just slightly smaller than the diameter of the baking pan.

Place the dough in the prepared pan and press evenly to the sides of the pan, making sure that the thickness of the dough is even. Flute the edges. Bake for 30–35 minutes, or until a rich golden brown, and up to 40 minutes for a crisper, crumblier shortbread. Remove from the oven.

Carefully run a sharp knife around the edges of the pan to loosen the shortbread then open and lift off the outer ring of the springform pan. Slide the shortbread off of the bottom of the pan onto a serving plate. Carefully slide a long cake spatula between the bottom of the shortbread and the parchment paper, sliding the spatula around until the shortbread is loosened completely from the paper then slide out the parchment paper and discard. While the shortbread is still warm, score the top into serving pieces with a sharp knife; this will guarantee that your slices are nice and neat once cooled.

When the shortbread has cooled, using a sharp knife, separate the slices of shortbread into thin wedges to serve.

Orange-Cranberry Spiced Granola with Almonds

Makes about 10 cups (about 2 1/2 l)

4 cups old-fashioned gluten-free rolled oats

1 1/2 cups (7 ounces / 190 g) slivered almonds, or coarsely chopped blanched hazelnuts or pecans

1 1/2 cups (7 ounces / 190 g) mixed seeds and grains of your choice (pumpkin, sunflower, flax, and sesame seeds)

1 1/2 to 2 teaspoons ground cinnamon

1/2 teaspoon ground ginger

1/2 teaspoon ground nutmeg

1/4 teaspoon salt

2 oranges, zested and juiced, about 3/4 cup (185 ml) juice

3/8 cup (scant 100 ml) vegetable oil

1/8 cup (25 ml) sesame oil

1/2 cup (125 ml) pure maple syrup, honey, or a combination

1 1/2 cups (7 ounces / 200 g) dried cranberries, cherries, or blueberries, or chopped candied orange peel, or a combination

HOMEMADE GRANOLA IS SO MUCH EASIER to make than you think. Just stir the ingredients together and bake—it's so easy to adapt to your own taste and what you have on hand. For a tropical-flavored granola, add chopped candied pineapple, orange, and lemon instead of dried berries, and toss in dried coconut flakes. Raisins, chopped dates, figs, or prunes make for an exotic treat. You could also add coarsely chopped or grated dark or milk chocolate. To heighten the orange flavor, whisk a few drops of orange oil or extract or 1 or 2 teaspoons orange blossom water into the liquid ingredients. And you can change out some of the oats for another flaked whole grain such as quinoa or spelt, if you prefer.

Granola on yogurt with fresh orange supremes and berries is a perfect treat. Scoop it onto ice cream, sprinkle it on fresh fruit, or scatter some on my Vanilla-Star Anise Poached Orange Slices (page 166) instead of crumble. Or serve it for breakfast with hot or cold milk or use it to top oatmeal or another hot cereal.

Preheat oven to 325 degrees F (180 degrees C) and line a large baking sheet with parchment paper.

Measure the oats into a large mixing bowl. Add the nuts, seeds and grains, cinnamon, ginger, nutmeg, and salt; toss and stir until well-combined.

In another bowl, whisk together the orange zest, juice, oils, and maple syrup until combined and the zest is no longer in clumps. Pour the liquid ingredients over the oat mixture and stir until evenly moistened and well-coated. Spread the granola mixture in a thin, even layer over the baking sheet.

Bake the granola for 30–35 minutes, carefully stirring every 10 minutes, making sure to push the granola from the outer edges in towards the center to avoid burning. Bake for a bit less time if you like chewier, moister granola, and a bit longer if you like dryer, crispier granola. The granola will continue to dry and clump as it cools, so if in doubt, remove from the oven sooner than later.

Allow the granola to cool completely before pouring into a clean bowl. Add the dried fruit to the granola and toss to evenly distribute. Store in an airtight container for up to two weeks.

Cakes

CAKE

2 medium to medium-large juice
   oranges

1 1/2 cups (7 ounces / 200 g)
   all-purpose flour

1 1/2 teaspoons baking powder

1/4 teaspoon salt (increase to
   1/2 teaspoon if using unsalted
   butter)

8 ounces (230 g) granulated
   sugar, either white or brown

16 tablespoons (8 ounces / 230 g)
   salted butter, melted and
   cooled

4 large eggs

ORANGE SYRUP

2/3 cup (165 ml) freshly squeezed
   and strained orange juice

2 tablespoons granulated sugar,
   either white or brown

Isabelle's Orange Cake

MY FRIEND ISABELLE'S FRENCH GRANDMOTHER was the first in
her family to make this simple, homey, yet luscious orange cake. The recipe was
then handed down from mother to daughter, through four generations, and is
now made by Isabelle and her daughter Clementine. The warm syrup permeates
the cake, leaving it dense and moist, yet never wet—the perfect, most satisfying
texture possible. Lovely eaten as is, but drizzle some orange-infused chocolate
ganache, fresh apricot compote, or pile on Marmalade Whipped Cream (page
159) just before serving to elevate it from comforting to elegant.

Cake

Preheat oven to 350 degrees F (180 degrees C). Butter the bottom and sides of
a 9-inch (23 cm) round baking pan and line the bottom with lightly buttered
parchment paper. Flour the bottom and sides of the pan, shaking out the excess,
and set aside.

   Finely zest and juice the 2 oranges; you should have about 1 tablespoon
plus 1 teaspoon zest and 2/3 to 3/4 cup (165 to 185 ml) juice.

   Combine the flour, baking powder, and salt together in a small bowl.

   In a large mixing bowl, stir together the sugar and butter until blended
and smooth. Stir in the eggs, 1 at a time, beating vigorously after each addition.
Stir the dry ingredients into the wet in 4 additions until well-combined and
lump-free after each addition, scraping down the sides of the bowl as needed.
Stir in the zest and juice until blended.

   Pour the batter into the prepared pan and bake for 30–35 minutes until
the center is just set and the cake is golden.

(continued)

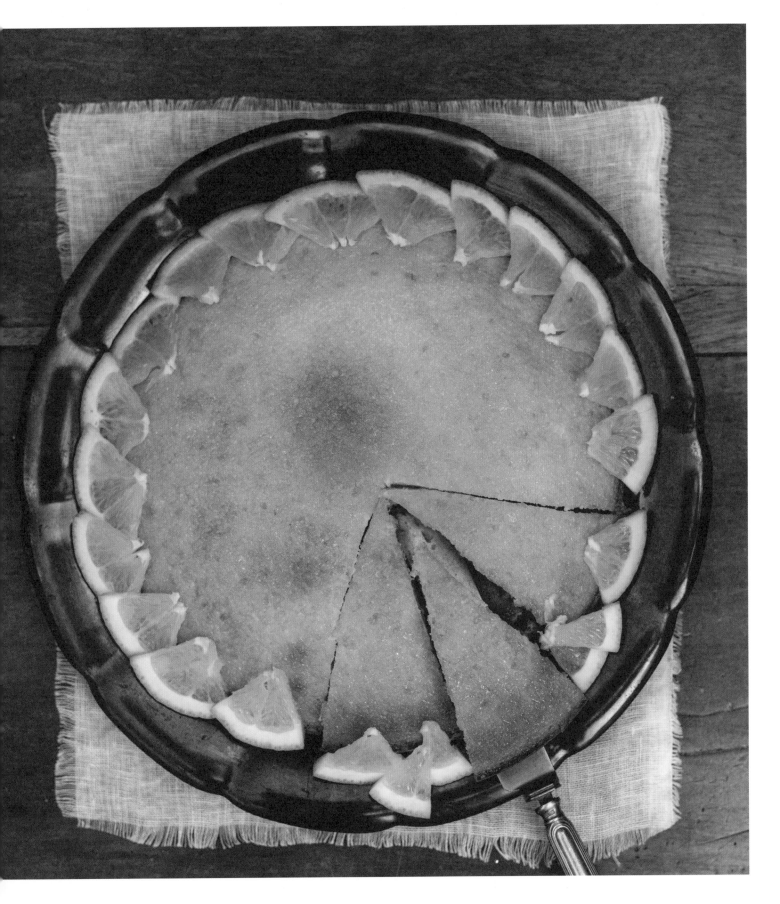

Orange Syrup

While the cake is baking, prepare the Orange Syrup by gently heating the orange juice and sugar together in a small saucepan over low heat just until all of the sugar has dissolved and the syrup is warm. This should only take 1–2 minutes at most. Remove from heat and set aside.

When the cake is done, remove it from the oven and run a sharp knife around the edge to loosen. Invert the cake onto a cooling rack, removing and discarding the parchment paper, then invert again, bottom down onto a cake platter. Immediately spoon the syrup evenly over the top of the hot cake, allowing some to drip down the sides and making sure the entire surface of the cake is infused with the syrup. Allow the cake to cool completely before serving.

Glazed Blood Orange Yogurt Loaf Cake

Makes 1 (9-inch / 23 cm)
loaf cake

LOAF CAKE

1 1/2 cups (7 ounces / 195 g) all-purpose flour

2 teaspoons baking powder

1/4 teaspoon salt

1 cup (250 ml) unsweetened plain whole-milk or Greek yogurt

1 cup (200 g) granulated white sugar

3 large eggs

3 blood oranges, zested

1/2 teaspoon vanilla extract

1/2 cup (125 ml) vegetable oil

BLOOD ORANGE SYRUP

1/3 cup (85 ml) blood orange juice

1 tablespoon granulated white sugar

GLAZE

2 tablespoons blood orange juice

1 cup (135 g) confectioners' sugar

THANKS TO THE YOGURT AND THE VEGETABLE OIl, this spectacular, intensely orange loaf cake stays moist for several days. Some friends even say that the cake should be allowed to "age" for 24 hours with the syrup before glazing and serving. The sweet orange glaze is optional; leave it off for a perfect breakfast or tea cake, or add the glaze for a more festive, special treat.

Loaf Cake

Preheat oven to 350 degrees F (180 degrees C). Butter a standard 9 x 5 x 2 1/2-inch (22 x 13 x 6 1/2 cm) or 8-cup (2 l) loaf pan, line the bottom with parchment paper, and flour the sides of the pan.

Sift or whisk together the flour, baking powder, and salt and set aside.

In a large mixing bowl, whisk together the yogurt, sugar, eggs, zest, and vanilla until blended and smooth. Slowly whisk the dry ingredients into the wet ingredients just until combined and smooth. Fold the oil into the batter, a little at a time, until well-blended and no oil has collected around the edges of the batter.

Pour the batter into the prepared pan and bake for 45–50 minutes, or until the center of the cake is moist but set and a tester inserted into the cake comes out clean.

(continued)

Blood Orange Syrup

Prepare the orange syrup by placing the orange juice and sugar in a small saucepan over low heat. Cook until warm and the sugar has completely dissolved and the liquid is clear. Set aside to cool slightly.

When the cake is done, remove from the oven onto a cooling rack that has been placed on top of a large foil-lined baking sheet and allow to cool for 10 minutes. Carefully loosen the cake from the pan by running a knife around the edges. Turn the cake out of the pan, discard the parchment paper, and then place the cake upright on the cooling rack. While the cake is still warm, pour and brush the warm syrup all over the top, allowing it to soak the loaf and run down the sides. Allow to cool completely.

Glaze

Prepare the glaze by stirring the orange juice into the sugar until the sugar has dissolved and the glaze is smooth. The glaze should be thin enough to spoon or drizzle over the cake but just stiff enough that some of the glaze will cling to the sides.

Gently lift the cake off of the rack and onto a serving platter.

Chocolate Orange Marble Loaf Cake

Makes 1 (9-inch / 23 cm)
loaf cake

1 3/4 cups (8 ounces / 230 g) all-purpose flour

2 teaspoons baking powder

1/4 teaspoon salt

12 tablespoons (6 ounces / 175 g) unsalted butter, softened to room temperature

1 1/8 cups (225 g) granulated white sugar

4 large eggs, at room temperature

3 tablespoons olive oil

1 large orange, zested

1 tablespoon freshly squeezed orange juice

2 tablespoons milk

1/4 teaspoon vanilla extract

2 packed tablespoons (18 g) unsweetened cocoa powder

THIS IS A SCRUMPTIOUS LOAF CAKE using a mix of butter for richness and olive oil for lightness, moistness, and flavor. This recipe is so simple to make and so truly delicious that it will quickly become a favorite to enjoy with family as well as when friends drop by. Drizzle Chocolate Orange Ganache (page 152) over the top for an extra-special treat.

Preheat oven to 350 degrees F (180 degrees C). Butter a standard 9 x 5 x 2 1/2-inch (23 x 13 x 6 1/2 cm) or 8-cup (2 l) loaf pan; fit a piece of parchment paper into the bottom.

Stir together the flour, baking powder, and salt in a small bowl.

Cream the butter and sugar together in a large mixing bowl, beating until light and fluffy. Beat in the eggs, 1 at a time, and then beat in the oil. Beat in the flour mixture until blended, scraping down the sides of the bowl.

Divide the batter evenly between 2 bowls. Beat the zest and juice into 1 portion of the batter, and the milk, vanilla, and cocoa into the other portion of batter until well-blended.

Spoon large dollops of each mixture, alternating the batters, into the prepared loaf pan. Drag a skewer or a long, sharp knife blade back and forth through the batter in swirls to create a marble pattern. Smooth the surface if necessary.

Bake for 55–60 minutes, until the cake is set in the center and just barely beginning to pull away from the sides of the pan. Cover the top of the cake loosely with a sheet of foil for the last 5–10 minutes of baking time to avoid overbrowning, if necessary.

Allow to cool in the pan for about 10 minutes before sliding a knife around the edges to loosen the cake and turning it out onto a cooling rack. Remove parchment paper from the bottom, allowing the cake to cool, top side up, on the rack.

Chocolate Orange Sponge Cake with Chocolate Orange Ganache

Makes 1 (10-inch / 25 cm) cake

CHOCOLATE ORANGE SPONGE CAKE

1 1/4 cups (scant 6 ounces / 165 g) all-purpose flour

1/4 cup (1 ounce / 25 g) cocoa powder

1 teaspoon baking powder

Scant 1/2 teaspoon salt

6 large eggs, separated

3 drops lemon juice, optional

1 1/4 cups (250 g) granulated white sugar

1/2 teaspoon vanilla extract

1/2 teaspoon Orange Extract (page 22)

1 orange, zested

1/4 cup (65 ml) cold water

1/4 cup (65 ml) freshly squeezed orange juice

CHOCOLATE ORANGE GANACHE

3/4 cup (3 1/2 ounces / 100 g) coarsely chopped orange-infused 70 percent dark chocolate, such as Lindt Excellence Orange Intense

1/2 cup (125 ml) heavy cream

WHEN WE CRAVE SOMETHING INTENSELY CHOCOLATE, we often turn to the dense, heavy, and rich. Break the spell with something light, moist, and ethereal, yet still satisfyingly chocolate—a sponge cake with the heavenly darkness of chocolate to soothe the soul, brightened with the essence of orange to lift the spirit.

Chocolate Orange Sponge Cake

Preheat oven to 325 degrees F (170 degrees C). Have ready an ungreased 10-inch (25 cm) tube pan with removable bottom and tube.

Sift the flour, cocoa, baking powder, and salt into a small bowl; stir to blend. Set aside.

Place the egg whites in a medium mixing bowl—plastic is preferable to glass—and add the lemon juice and a small pinch of salt to help stabilize the whites; set aside. Place the egg yolks in a large mixing bowl, and beat on high speed until thick and pale. Add the sugar and continue beating until very thick and creamy. Beat in the vanilla and orange extracts and the zest.

Add the dry ingredients to the yolk mixture in 3 additions, alternating with the cold water and orange juice in 2 additions, beating after each addition until blended, scraping down the sides of the bowl as necessary.

Using very clean beaters, beat the whites on low speed for 30 seconds, increasing the speed to high and continue beating until the whites are very dense and stiff peaks hold.

(continued)

Gently fold $1/3$ of the whites into the batter to lighten the heavy batter so as not to break or deflate the whites. Then fold in another $1/3$, and then the remaining whites. Make sure there are no pockets or lumps of whites left, yet try not to overmix the batter.

Pour into the tube pan and bake for 50–55 minutes until set. Press very lightly on the surface of the cake, it should be light yet set; if an indentation remains and the cake hisses when pressed—as if the batter is still a mousse and not yet set— allow the cake to bake for an extra few minutes.

Invert the pan to cool the cake upside down. Once the cake is cool, run a knife with a long blade around the sides and around the center tube to loosen. Lift the tube and cake out from the outer pan. Run a knife carefully underneath the cake to loosen from the bottom of the cake pan all around. Very carefully turn over, lift out the center tube, then turn the cake upright onto a serving platter.

Chocolate Orange Ganache

Place the chocolate into a medium heatproof mixing bowl. Slowly heat the cream in a small saucepan until it comes just to the boiling point. Pour the cream immediately over the chocolate and stir until it is smooth and creamy. Allow the ganache to cool to room temperature, stirring occasionally, until thickened to a drizzling consistency before spooning over the sponge cake.

Orange-Honey Spiced Pecan Cake with Cream Cheese Frosting

Makes 1 (8-inch / 20 cm)
2-layer cake

CAKE

3 medium to large oranges

1 cup (3 ounces / 85 g) quick cooking oats

8 tablespoons (4 ounces / 115 g) unsalted butter, cubed and softened to room temperature, plus more to prepare pans

1 cup (5 ounces / 135 g) all-purpose flour, sifted

1 teaspoon baking powder

1/2 teaspoon baking soda

1/2 teaspoon salt

1 teaspoon ground cinnamon

1/2 teaspoon ground allspice

1/4 teaspoon ground nutmeg

3/4 cup (150 g) granulated white sugar

1/2 cup (125 ml) honey

1/2 cup (125 ml) maple syrup

2 large eggs

1 teaspoon vanilla extract

1 cup (3 1/2 ounces / 100 g) coarsely chopped pecans or walnuts

(continued)

THIS IS AN ASTONISHING CAKE ENVELOPED IN RUSTIC comfort. Similar to the warm spice flavors and dense, super moist texture of a carrot cake, but without the carrots, this cake needs nothing more than tangy cream cheese frosting, the perfect foil to the sweet cake and the earthy pecans. Decorate by scattering some chopped candied orange zest and more pecans, by lightly dusting the top of the frosted cake with Orange Sugar (page 21), or by adding some Candied Orange Slices (page 192) in a lovely pattern. If you prefer, you can use a 9 x 13-inch (22 x 33 cm) cake pan or a cupcake tin, baking for closer to 30 minutes.

Cake

Finely zest 2 of the oranges and set aside. Juice all of the oranges for 1 cup (250 ml) juice. In a small saucepan, bring the juice just to a boil. Remove from heat.

Place the oats in a medium mixing bowl and pour the hot juice over the oats, stirring until moistened. Let stand for 30 minutes.

Preheat oven to 325 degrees F (170 degrees C). Butter and flour 2 (8-inch / 20 cm) round cake pans, tapping out the excess flour, and line the bottoms with parchment paper. In a small bowl, stir together the flour, baking powder, baking soda, salt, cinnamon, allspice, and nutmeg.

In a large mixing bowl, beat butter and sugar together on low speed until light and fluffy. Continue beating, adding the honey and syrup in a slow, steady stream. Beat in the eggs, 1 at a time, just until blended. Add the zest and vanilla, and then beat in the oats, followed by the dry ingredients, beating just until well-blended. Fold in the pecans.

(continued)

12 tablespoons (6 ounces / 170 g)
    unsalted butter, softened

8 ounces (225 g) cream cheese,
    at room temperature

1 teaspoon vanilla extract

1/8 teaspoon Orange Extract
    (page 22)

3 to 4 cups (375 to 500 g)
    confectioners' sugar, divided

Pour the batter into the prepared pans and bake for about 35–40 minutes until the layers are just set in the center.

Allow the cake to cool in the pans for 10 minutes before carefully sliding the blade of a knife around the edges and turning them out onto cooling racks, peeling off and discarding the parchment paper, inverting top side up, and cooling completely before frosting.

Cream Cheese Frosting

In a large mixing bowl, beat the butter and cream cheese together until well-blended and creamy. Beat in the vanilla and orange extracts. Beat in 3 cups (375 g) sugar. If a sweeter, firmer frosting is desired, beat in the remaining sugar. Frost the tops of the 2 layers with 1/3 of the frosting each; place 1 layer on top of the other and use the rest of the frosting to cover the sides of the cake. You can serve the cake as is, or decorate with candied orange zest or slices.

Caramelized Orange Cardamom Upside-Down Cake

Makes 1 (8 1/2-inch / 22 cm) round cake

8 tablespoons (4 ounces / 120 g) unsalted butter, softened to room temperature, divided

1/2 cup (3 1/2 ounces / 100 g) firmly packed brown sugar, light or dark

Pinch of ground nutmeg

Pinch of ground cardamom

2 naval or other large oranges

3/4 cup (150 g) granulated white sugar

2 large eggs

1/2 teaspoon vanilla extract

2 teaspoons baking powder

1/2 teaspoon salt

1/16 teaspoon ground nutmeg

1/8 teaspoon ground cardamom

1 1/4 cups plus 2 tablespoons (6 1/2 ounces / 185 g) all-purpose flour

1/2 cup (125 ml) milk

I HAVE BEEN MAKING CARAMELIZED UPSIDE-DOWN CAKE with this recipe for at least twenty-five years, the original recipe having been ripped out of a French cooking magazine. Over the years, the recipe has been adjusted, readjusted, and fine-tuned with spices and flavorings added, and the fruit changed. Throughout the year, I make this deliciously simple cake with seasonal peaches, plums, berries, cranberries, and pears. And now oranges. Pinches of warm spices like nutmeg and cardamom, or cinnamon if you prefer, add nice warmth and depth to the cake flavors while the zest stirred into the batter intensifies the orange flavor. There is something quite festive about the orange-spice-caramel combination even if the cake is perfect comfort food.

Preheat oven to 425 degrees F (220 degrees C). Have ready a deep, round nonstick cake pan 8 1/2 to 8 3/4 inches (22 to 23 cm).

In a medium mixing bowl, beat 4 tablespoons (2 ounces / 60 g) butter with the brown sugar, nutmeg, and cardamom until smooth, blended, and creamy. Using a spatula or the back of a spoon, spread evenly in the bottom of the cake pan to the edges.

Zest 1 of the oranges and set aside. Peel the oranges, both outer peel and white pith, and dice the fruit into small chunks. If there is any runoff juice from the oranges from chopping, reserve and add to the batter. Spread the orange chunks evenly in the pan on top of the brown sugar mixture.

In a large mixing bowl, beat the remaining butter and the white sugar until smooth and creamy. Beat in the eggs, 1 at a time, beating briefly after each addition until blended; beat in the vanilla and reserved zest. In a small mixing bowl, stir the baking powder, salt, nutmeg, and cardamom into the flour, and then beat the flour into the batter in 3 additions alternating with the milk in 2 additions, scraping down the sides of the bowl as necessary. The batter should be well-blended, smooth, and creamy. Pour the batter into the cake pan over the oranges.

Bake for about 35 minutes, covering loosely with a square of aluminum foil after 20–25 minutes when the cake is browned. The cake is done when the center is set and firm and a tester inserted comes out clean. The caramel should be bubbling a bit around the edges.

Remove from the oven and allow to cool on a rack for 10 minutes. At the end of 10 minutes, carefully slide the blade of a knife around the edges of the cake to loosen, place a serving platter or cake plate upside down on top of the cake pan and flip the cake onto the platter, the caramel and oranges side up; gently lift off the pan. Allow to cool before serving.

Rye Spice Cake with Marmalade Whipped Cream and Orange Glaze

Makes 1 (8 1/2-inch / 22 cm) round cake

ORANGE MARMALADE WHIPPED CREAM

4 tablespoons cold water

1 teaspoon unflavored powdered gelatin

1 cup (250 ml) heavy whipping cream, chilled

1 tablespoon confectioners' sugar

2 tablespoons orange marmalade

(continued)

THIS SUBLIME AND UNUSUAL cake topped with caramel and mountains of marmalade whipped cream is a special treat. The lightly sweetened, orangey whipped cream is the perfect accompaniment to the delicate, earthy spiced rye cake and balances beautifully with the barely bitter edge of the glaze.

Orange Marmalade Whipped Cream

Prepare this whipped cream the day before baking and serving the cake, allowing it to chill and firm in the refrigerator. The addition of gelatin helps stabilize the whipped cream, giving it body and lightness as well as allowing it to last for 2 days in the refrigerator. Use a marmalade that is more jelly than rind.

Chill a mixing bowl and beaters in the refrigerator. Spoon the water into a small saucepan and sprinkle the gelatin over the water. Let the gelatin soften for 5 minutes. Place the saucepan on very low heat and heat gently for 4 minutes, never letting the water come to a boil, stirring and swirling the pan as needed, until the gelatin has dissolved. Remove from the heat and let cool for several minutes.

Pour the cream into the chilled bowl and beat until soft peaks form. Add the sugar and continue beating until the beaters leave visible traces in the cream. Add the gelatin water in a slow steady stream, poured down the side of the bowl, as you continue beating on medium-high speed until the cream is thick. Beat in the marmalade 1 tablespoon at a time. Chill the cream in the refrigerator until firm, several hours or overnight. Pile on top of the cake or pass around in a serving bowl.

(continued)

8 tablespoons (4 ounces / 120 g)
unsalted butter, softened to
room temperature, plus more
to prepare pan

3/4 cup (5 1/2 ounces / 155 g)
dark brown sugar

1 orange, finely zested

2 large eggs

1/2 teaspoon vanilla extract

1 cup (5 ounces / 135)
all-purpose or cake flour

1 cup (scant 4 1/2 ounces / 130 g)
light or white rye flour

1 teaspoon gingerbread spice

1/2 teaspoon ground cinnamon

1/2 teaspoon ground ginger

1/2 teaspoon ground anise seed

1/4 teaspoon ground nutmeg

1/4 teaspoon ground allspice

1 teaspoon Orange Powder
(page 19), optional

1 teaspoon baking powder

1/2 teaspoon baking soda

1 teaspoon salt

1/2 cup (125 ml) milk

1/4 cup (65 ml) orange juice

ORANGE GLAZE

1/4 cup (1.8 ounces / 50 g) dark
brown sugar

1 small orange, juiced, about
1/4 cup (65 ml)

1 tablespoon orange marmalade

1 tablespoon Grand Marnier or
Cointreau, optional

Rye Spice Cake

The rye flour used is neither a strong nor a dark rye, rather it is a light or white, soft rye with seven percent protein; don't substitute another flour for this as the rye does impart a distinct, if subtle, rye flavor to the cake. The addition of the gingerbread spice simply reinforces the flavors of the individual spices, but don't hesitate to replace it with an additional 1/4 teaspoon cinnamon, 1/4 teaspoon ground ginger, 1/8 teaspoon allspice, 1/8 teaspoon nutmeg, and 1/8 teaspoon ground cloves.

Preheat oven to 325 degrees F (170 degrees C). Butter the bottom and sides of an 8 1/2- or 9-inch (22 or 23 cm) springform pan and line the bottom with parchment paper.

In a large mixing bowl, cream butter, brown sugar, and zest together until blended and creamy. Beat in the eggs, 1 at a time, adding the vanilla with the second egg, just until blended, scraping down the bowl as needed. In a separate bowl, whisk the flours, spices, Orange Powder, if using, baking powder, baking soda, and salt together. Beat the dry ingredients into the batter in 3 additions alternating with the milk and then the orange juice, beginning and ending with the dry, and beating after each addition just until blended, scraping down the sides of the bowl as needed.

Pour the batter into the prepared pan and bake for about 30 minutes, or until set in the center. The cake should only start to pull away from the sides of the pan as it is taken out of the oven.

Cool the cake for 10 minutes in the pan before sliding the blade of a knife around the edge to loosen the cake, carefully opening and removing the outside ring and sliding the cake off of the parchment paper onto a cooling rack. Allow to cool completely before glazing and topping with the Orange Marmalade Whipped Cream.

Orange Glaze

Place all of the ingredients in a small saucepan and cook at a low rolling boil over low heat, whisking constantly, for 10 minutes until syrupy. Remove from heat to cool. Once the syrup has cooled and thickened slightly, drizzle or brush over the cake before serving.

Special Chocolate Orange Cake with Simple Buttercream Frosting

Makes 1 (9-inch / 23 cm) layer cake

CHOCOLATE ORANGE CAKE

1 3/4 cup (8 1/2 ounces / 240 g) all-purpose flour

2 cups (400 g) granulated white sugar

3/4 cup (2 1/2 ounces / 75 g) unsweetened cocoa powder

1 1/2 teaspoons baking powder

1 1/2 teaspoons baking soda

1/2 teaspoon ground cinnamon

1 teaspoon salt

2 large eggs

1 cup (250 ml) whole milk or buttermilk

1/2 cup (125 ml) vegetable oil

1 teaspoon vanilla extract

1 teaspoon Orange Extract (page 22)

1 orange, finely zested

1 cup (250 ml) orange juice, heated but not boiling

(continued)

A DENSE, SUPER MOIST CAKE that can only be described as *sinful,* this is a recipe that was handed down to me from my dad, a NASA engineer whose weekend passion was baking. I have been making his cake now for 30 years and almost always bake this for my own birthday. It's that special. Frost the layer cake with the buttercream frosting, or frost just the top and outside of the cake, and fill the cake with a cup or so of either orange curd or Orange Marmalade Whipped Cream (page 159) for an even more spectacular dessert.

Chocolate Orange Cake

Preheat oven to 350 degrees F (180 degrees C). Oil and flour 2 (9-inch / 23 cm) round cake pans generously; alternately, oil the pans and line the bottoms with parchment paper.

Combine the flour, sugar, cocoa, baking powder, baking soda, cinnamon, and salt in a large mixing bowl and whisk together to combine well. Add the eggs, milk, oil, vanilla and orange extracts, and zest. Beat on low until well-blended then increase speed to medium and beat for 2 minutes. Stir in the hot orange juice. The batter will be very runny. Carefully divide the batter between the prepared cake pans.

Bake for 35–40 minutes or until the center is set. Remove from the oven and allow to cool for 10–15 minutes in the pans before running a knife blade around the edges of the cakes to loosen, turning them out of the pans, discarding the parchment paper, and allowing them to cool completely, top side up, on cooling racks before frosting.

(continued)

CHOCOLATE ORANGE
BUTTERCREAM FROSTING

8 tablespoons (4 ounces / 120 g)
unsalted butter, softened

3 cups (13 ounces / 370 g)
confectioners' sugar

5 packed tablespoons (2 ounces /
60 g) unsweetened cocoa
powder

4 to 5 tablespoons hot, but not
boiling, orange juice

Chocolate Orange Buttercream Frosting

In a medium mixing bowl, beat the butter and sugar together. Add the cocoa and 4 tablespoons of hot juice and beat, scraping down the sides of the bowl as necessary, until well-blended and fluffy; add the additional tablespoon orange juice, if necessary. Chill in the refrigerator for desired spreading consistency, if necessary.

Desserts

Vanilla–Star Anise Poached Orange Slices with Gingerbread Oat Crumble

Serves 4 to 6

POACHED ORANGES

4 to 6 medium to medium-large oranges

1 1/4 cups (250 g) granulated white sugar

3/4 cup (185 ml) water

1/4 cup (65 ml) orange juice

1 vanilla bean

2 star anise

1 tablespoon Cointreau or Grand Marnier

GINGERBREAD OAT CRUMBLE

1/2 cup (2 1/2 ounces / 70 g) all-purpose or cake flour

1/4 cup (50 g) granulated white sugar

3/4 teaspoon gingerbread spice

1/16 teaspoon salt

5 tablespoons (2 1/2 ounces / 75 g) unsalted butter, chilled and cubed

1/3 cup (1.3 ounces / 35 g) oat bran

THIS IS AN EASILY ADAPTABLE DESSERT that can be made for 4, 6, or 8 by simply adding more oranges—although not more than 6 for this quantity syrup. Vanilla–Star Anise Poached Orange Slices topped with crunchy Gingerbread Oat Crumble is an elegant, luxurious yet simple dessert that can be made ahead of time, in the afternoon for an evening meal. Presentation of the poached oranges is more intriguing when you use a mix of navel, blood, and sweet Cara Cara or Maltaise oranges, dividing them up between the dessert plates and layering them by size and shades of pink, red, and orange. Drizzle syrup over the oranges, top with 2 or 3 tablespoons of the crumble and serve with a scoop of ice cream or a dollop of lightly sweetened whipped cream.

Poached Oranges

Peel the oranges and cut away all of the white pith and outer membrane. Slice each orange across the core into 1/4-inch (1/2 cm) slices, 6 per orange, reserving any juice that runs off. Push out and discard any spongy white core.

Place the sugar, water, orange juice, and any runoff juice from the sliced oranges into a large skillet or sauté pan. Slice the vanilla bean down the center not quite cutting all the way through. Scrape out some of the seeds with the tip of a sharp knife, and add both the bean and seeds, star anise, and Cointreau to the pan. Bring to a boil over medium heat, stirring often so the sugar dissolves. Gently slide the orange slices into the liquid, making sure that each slice is submerged. (You may need to poach the oranges in 2 batches.) Once the liquid returns to a boil, lower the heat to a low simmer and poach the oranges for 8 minutes.

(continued)

Using a slotted spoon, lift the orange slices from the pan onto a plate or platter to cool. Allow the liquid to simmer for an additional 10–12 minutes until reduced to a thickened sauce or syrup; if you simmered the orange slices in 2 batches, the reducing time will be less.

Remove the syrup from the heat and allow to cool before removing and discarding the vanilla pod and the star anise. Drizzle syrup over the oranges before topping with crumble.

Gingerbread Oat Crumble

Preheat oven to 350 degrees F (180 degrees C). Line a large baking sheet with aluminum foil.

Combine the flour, sugar, spice, and salt in a medium mixing bowl. Add the butter, tossing to coat in the dry ingredients. Using your thumb and fingertips, rub the butter into the dry ingredients until well-blended and there are no large chunks of butter left. Add the oat bran and combine thoroughly.

Spread the mixture in a fairly thin, even layer on the prepared baking sheet and bake for 12–15 minutes, or until golden. The crumble should be dry and crumbly when tossed with a fork. Remove from the oven and allow to cool before serving.

Store any extra crumble in an airtight plastic container in the refrigerator for up to 2 weeks. This crumble is delicious served on the poached fruit, as well as ice cream, fruit salads, or yogurt.

Wine-Poached Prunes with Orange and Cinnamon

10 1/2 ounces (300 g) moist pitted prunes (weighed without pits, about 45 to 50 prunes)

1/4 cup (50 g) granulated white sugar

1/8 teaspoon cinnamon

1/2-inch (1 cm) thick orange slice with peel

2 cups (500 ml) liquid—1/4 cup (65 ml) red wine plus 1/2 cup (125 ml) orange juice plus 1 1/4 cups (310 ml) cold water or replace 1/4 cup (65 ml) of water with more wine

DON'T LET THE WORD *PRUNES* FOOL YOU. Your grandma's stewed prunes these most definitely are not. This is a beautiful recipe, crazy in its simplicity, yet sensual and intriguing in texture and flavor; a very adult twist on my father's prune and apricot compote. I simmered the prunes in Recioto della Valpolicella Classico, which may be the only real red dessert wine in the world, although any full-bodied fruity red wine or port wine will do.

Glistening, slippery wine-poached prunes that burst on the tongue make a sensational dessert served simply with whipped cream or ice cream or a simple pound cake drizzled with the luxurious syrup. However, these poached prunes are also a delicious accompaniment to roast meat; simply increase the amount of red wine to water, as indicated.

Place the prunes, sugar, cinnamon, orange slice, and liquid in a saucepan, bring to a boil, lower the heat and simmer 10–15 minutes until the prunes are plump and tender but have not exploded. Using a slotted spoon, carefully remove the prunes from the liquid to a bowl and continue to simmer the liquid with the orange slice until reduced by about half, another 12–15 minutes. The liquid will thicken as it cools. Discard the orange slice.

Serve the prunes warm in a bowl with some of the syrup and topped with whipped cream or ice cream, if you like.

Moroccan-Spiced Orange Slices in Orange Blossom Water

Serves 4 to 5

5 medium to large navel or large blood oranges

3 tablespoons orange blossom water

1 teaspoon ground cinnamon

2 tablespoons confectioners' sugar

1/2 pomegranate, seeded

1 1/2 to 2 tablespoons coarsely chopped unsalted pistachios

8 to 10 mint leaves, chopped or torn, for garnish

THIS TRADITIONAL NORTH AFRICAN DESSERT—to which I've added pomegranate seeds for tartness, pistachios for crunch, and mint for a bright touch—is a light, surprisingly refreshing and fragrant finale to a hearty, rich, or spicy meal; a tagine, couscous, stew, or grill. Or serve it on a warm summer afternoon or evening for a cool, sophisticated, intriguing treat.

For 2 or 3 people, use 3 oranges and half all of the other ingredients. Orange blossom water, also known as orange flower water, can be purchased in Lebanese, Indian, Middle-Eastern, or gourmet food shops.

Peel the oranges and cut away all of the white pith and outer membrane. Slice each orange across the core into 1/4-inch (1/2 cm) slices, 6 per orange, reserving any juice that runs off. Push out and discard any spongy white core. Fan the slices in concentric circles, slightly overlapping the fruit, on a large round serving platter.

Drizzle the orange blossom water and any reserved runoff juice over the fruit. Using a fine sieve, lightly and evenly dust with cinnamon and a generous sprinkling of sugar. Chill the oranges for at least 1 hour or longer in the refrigerator before serving.

When ready to serve, sprinkle the pomegranate seeds, pistachios, and mint leaves evenly over the top.

Oranges in Spiced Wine Syrup

Serves 6

6 large navel, Cara Cara, or blood oranges

2 cups (500 ml) dry, fruity red wine

1 orange, juiced, about 1/2 cup (125 ml)

1 1/2 cups (300 g) granulated white sugar

1/4 teaspoon ground cinnamon

1 strip orange zest, about 1/2 x 3 inches (1 x 7 cm) long

1 strip lemon zest, about 1/4 to 1/2 x 2 inches (1 x 5 cm) long

3 star anise

1 whole vanilla bean

2 (1-inch / 2 cm) cubes candied ginger, each cut into 8 small cubes

THIS IS A STUNNING AND IMPRESSIVE DESSERT redolent of winter holidays and festive occasions. Oranges bathed in wine syrup is a traditional Spanish treat made with a rich, dry, and fruity red wine such as a Rioja. I have enhanced the orange flavor by blending the wine with juice, vanilla, orange and lemon zest, cinnamon, star anise, and candied ginger to add warmth and complexity to the syrup, creating something reminiscent of hot mulled wine.

I used a Spanish Rioja, but the recipe will work well with any dry, fruity wine such as a Pinot Noir, Chianti, a robust Cabernet Franc, or a French Burgundy. If there is any leftover syrup, simply use it to poach more orange slices or pour over fresh orange slices. The syrup can also be spooned over ice cream, blended with Champagne or sparkling white wine for a kir (apéritif), drizzled on a cake or the Orange, Ricotta, and Chèvre Tart (page 184), or even stirred into meat juices for a sweet and savory sauce.

Peel the oranges with a sharp knife, removing the top and bottom ends, white pith, and outer membrane. If poaching and serving the oranges whole, the top and bottom of each should be flat, allowing the orange to sit firmly on either end. I find that halving the oranges, cutting across the core, or cutting into 4 thick slices makes for easier eating.

Pour the wine and orange juice into a deep saucepan wide enough to hold the 6 oranges comfortably. Whisk in the sugar and cinnamon, add the orange and lemon zest, star anise, vanilla bean, and ginger. Bring up to a boil over medium heat then reduce the heat slightly and boil for 5 minutes—it should be a rolling boil but never foam.

Using a slotted spoon, lower the whole, halved, or sliced oranges into the boiling liquid. Keeping at a low rolling boil, continue cooking for 15 minutes, turning the whole oranges every 3–4 minutes to ensure even poaching; the cut oranges need no turning if submerged in the liquid and should cook for closer to 10 minutes. Remove the oranges to a serving plate or bowl and continue cooking the wine for just 10 minutes more until it is reduced and syrupy.

(continued)

Remove pan from the heat and allow the syrup to cool to room temperature; it will continue to thicken as it cools.

To serve, place the oranges in a deep serving platter. Remove the zests, vanilla bean, and star anise from the syrup before pouring over the oranges. Serve each orange in a wide soup or dessert bowl, spooning syrup over the fruit. Serve with a sharp knife, a fork, and a spoon for the syrup. Top with freshly whipped cream or a scoop of vanilla ice cream, if you like.

Orange Aspic with Summer Berries

1 to 2 small oranges

2 cups (500 ml) orange juice

1/2 cup (100 g) granulated white sugar

1 star anise

10 mint leaves or 6 small flowering branches lemon thyme, each about 3 inches (7 1/2 cm) long

1/2 lime, juiced, about 2 teaspoons

3 1/2 teaspoons (10 g) unflavored powdered gelatin

1/2 cup (125 ml) cold water

10 1/2 to 14 ounces (300 to 400 g) berries of choice, or a mix of blueberries, raspberries, and blackberries, or small strawberries

MAKE THESE LIGHT, FRUITY, AND REFRESHING ASPICS the day before serving; the perfect end to a light summer repast or a rich winter meal. Using more fruit, a mix of orange supremes and berries, will give you 8 individual desserts with more fruit to aspic, less fruit will give you 6 individual desserts with more aspic to fruit, both equally delicious. These are beauties whether unmolded onto dessert plates or served in wine glasses or pretty transparent dessert bowls. They are delicious served with a dollop of freshly whipped cream.

Pare 1 wide, long strip of peel from 1 of the oranges with a vegetable peeler. Place the strip of peel, orange juice, sugar, star anise, mint leaves, and lime juice in a medium nonreactive saucepan.

In a small bowl, sprinkle the gelatin over the water, gently tapping to push it under the liquid, and leave for 5 minutes. Begin heating the orange juice mixture over low heat, making sure that the juice never comes to the boil, but remains very hot and just steaming.

When the gelatin has softened, add it to the hot spiced orange juice and heat for 5 minutes, stirring with a whisk, never letting the juice come to a simmer. Remove from the heat and cool to room temperature.

Clean the berries, trim the strawberries, and peel and cut the oranges into supremes. Rinse the individual molds or verrines with cold water and shake out excess water without wiping dry. Divide the berries and orange supremes between the molds. When the aspic liquid has cooled, strain the liquid through a fine sieve and divide evenly among the molds, pouring it over the fruit.

Chill overnight. To unmold simply dip the bottom half of the mold briefly in a bowl of hot water or hold just the bottom under hot running water for a few seconds; slide the blade of a knife around the outside of the aspic to loosen then unmold onto individual dessert plates just before serving. Top with whipped cream and a few more berries, of course.

Oven-Roasted Vanilla, Blood Orange, and Rhubarb Compote

Serves 4 to 6

16 ounces (455 g) rhubarb or a bit more

1 vanilla bean

6 large or 7 small blood oranges or a mix of blood and sweet oranges

2 tablespoons Demerara, granulated brown, or turbinado sugar

THE WOMAN IN ROOM #19, MICHELLE H., stayed at the hotel for two weeks our first summer at the Diderot. She had come up from the south of France to meet her very first boyfriend, her first love, whom she hadn't seen or spoken to in fifty years. My staff and I watched a beautiful romance unfold, two teens got to know each other again after five decades apart, and a flame reignited. A vivacious, charming woman, Michelle and I spent a lot of time chatting—she loved having someone to whom she could recount and discuss her wonderfully romantic story. In the course of our talks, I told her about this cookbook and she enthusiastically offered to send me the recipe for one of her favorite desserts, this oven-roasted rhubarb and blood orange compote.

I made some changes to Michelle's recipe to highlight the oranges and bring out more of the orange essence, hidden under the strong taste of the rhubarb in the original instructions. I love this flavorful, summery compote using all blood oranges or mixing tarter blood oranges with sweeter Navelina, Lane Late, or Cara Cara oranges. If you cannot find blood oranges, try and find red navels or pink Cara Cara for their beautiful color. A scrumptious compote to eat sweet or savory, over ice cream, a simple pound or sponge cake, or with grilled or roasted meat.

Preheat oven to 400 degrees F (200 degrees C). Have ready a rimmed baking sheet or baking dish large enough to hold all of the fruit in a single layer.

Trim and wash the rhubarb stalks and cut into 1-inch (2 1/2 cm) chunks. Spread the rhubarb on the baking sheet in a single layer. Slice the vanilla bean down the center and add it to the rhubarb.

Remove the peel and white pith from 4 of the oranges and slice each orange into 6 slices; add the slices to the rhubarb. Juice the remaining 2–3 oranges for 3/4 cup (185 ml) juice and pour over the fruit. Sprinkle the sugar evenly over the top.

Bake until the rhubarb is very tender, about 20 minutes, leaving the fruit in the oven for an additional 2–3 minutes if you prefer the fruit softer and a finer compote. Remove from the oven and allow to cool for a few minutes before discarding the vanilla bean and mashing the fruit as much or as little as you like and spooning into a bowl.

Serve the compote warm or at room temperature. Any leftover compote should be refrigerated, and is delicious served chilled.

Orange Riz au Lait

1 cup (7 ounces / 200 g)
   uncooked short-grain rice

4 to 5 tablespoons (60 to 75 g)
   granulated white sugar, divided

1/8 teaspoon salt

1 small orange, very finely zested
   and juiced (at least 1/3 cup /
   80 ml)

1 vanilla bean or 1 teaspoon
   vanilla extract

3 1/4 cups (750 ml) whole milk, or
   half milk and half cream

1 tablespoon (1/2 ounce / 15 g)
   unsalted butter

RIZ AU LAIT, THE FRENCH VERSION OF RICE PUDDING, is rice cooked down in milk and then heavily sweetened. It is a simple, weighty, and inexpensive snack an older generation of French women fed their children to insulate them against the cold and damp of winter, or to simply add on the pounds, an old-fashioned way to help them grow faster and protect their bodies against sickness. This classic nursery treat is still to this day my husband's most loved comfort food, which stirs up fond memories of his childhood—warm, soothing, and cozy.

This orange version tastes like a warm Creamsicle, delicate and delicious. Add a few drops of orange essence or extract to the pudding for a stronger orange flavor, or a few drops of orange blossom water for a warmer, more complex flavor, if you like.

Place the rice in a fine-mesh sieve and rinse under running water until the water runs clear. Then place in a medium saucepan, cover with water, and bring to a boil; allow to boil 5 minutes and then drain.

Clean the pan and add the rice back, along with 1 tablespoon sugar, salt, and zest. Slice the vanilla bean down the center and scrape out the seeds, adding both the pod and the seeds to the pan. Pour the milk over the rice, stir, and place over medium heat. Bring it just up to a boil and then immediately turn down to as low a heat as possible. Cover the saucepan, leaving it slightly ajar, and allow the pudding to simmer for 25–35 minutes, stirring often so the rice neither sticks to the bottom of the pan nor bubbles up and over. Cooking time will depend on the type and quality of the rice you are using.

The pudding is done when the rice has absorbed almost all of the liquid and is very tender, almost melting in the mouth; riz au lait rice should not be al dente, the pudding should be thick and very creamy and not dry.

Remove the saucepan from the heat and carefully remove and discard the vanilla bean. Add the butter and 3 tablespoons of the remaining sugar and stir until the butter is melted and well-blended into the rice. Carefully but vigorously stir in the orange juice gradually until well-blended. Taste and add the last tablespoon of sugar if you want the pudding sweeter. Spoon into 6 dessert bowls and serve warm or cooled, as is or topped with lightly sweetened whipped cream.

Orange Panna Cotta
with Orange Compote

PANNA COTTA

2 1/2 cups (625 ml) heavy or light cream, divided

2 teaspoons (1/4 ounce / 7 g) unflavored powdered gelatin

1/2 cup (100 g) granulated white sugar

1/2 cup (125 ml) orange juice

1 teaspoon finely grated orange zest

2 tablespoons whiskey

1/2 teaspoon vanilla extract

1/4 teaspoon Orange Extract (page 22) or orange blossom water

ORANGE COMPOTE

2 medium to large oranges

3 teaspoons granulated brown sugar or honey

1/4 teaspoon vanilla extract

PANNA COTTA, COOKED CREAM IN ITALIAN, is a smooth, creamy sumptuous dessert that seems much more difficult to make than it really is. Simply whisk, heat, chill, and it's done. The combination of orange, whiskey, and vanilla is so delicious, delicate, and intriguing, and the compote adds a fresh, fruity intensity to a truly luxurious treat.

Panna Cotta

Pour 1 cup (250 ml) of the cream into a medium heavy-bottom saucepan and sprinkle the gelatin on top; gently tap the gelatin to push it under the liquid. Allow to sit for 5 minutes. Place the saucepan on a low heat and allow the cream to heat slowly, whisking gently, for 4–5 minutes until the gelatin dissolves completely; do not allow the cream to come to a boil.

Whisk in the sugar, remaining cream, orange juice, and zest. Continue to cook over low heat until the sugar has dissolved and the liquid is thoroughly warmed through. Stir in the whiskey and vanilla and orange extracts. Remove from the heat.

Divide evenly between 6 glasses, pudding bowls, or verrines and cover with plastic wrap; refrigerate overnight.

Orange Compote

Cut away the peel, white pith, and outer membrane from the oranges. Cut the fruit into small cubes for about 2 cups (500 ml) fruit. Place the fruit, brown sugar, and vanilla in a sauté pan and heat at a low simmer for 5 minutes, stirring with a wooden spoon. Remove from the heat, pour into a bowl, and allow to cool to room temperature. When ready to serve, spoon a heaping tablespoon of orange compote on top of each panna cotta. Top with lightly sweetened and whipped cream, if desired.

A Summery Cherry, Berry, Citrus, and Basil Cobbler

Serves 9

FILLING

- 4 cups pitted, halved cherries
- 2 cups blueberries
- 1/3 cup (65 g) granulated white sugar
- 1 1/2 tablespoons (14 g) cornstarch
- 1/2 cup (125 ml) orange juice
- Scant 1/8 teaspoon salt
- 1/4 teaspoon vanilla extract
- 1 tablespoon apple cider or balsamic vinegar
- 8 to 10 plump basil leaves, finely chopped or sliced into thin strips

ALTHOUGH ORANGES ARE WINTER FRUIT and berries embody the very essence of summer, the delectable combination of the two makes me wonder how it is they don't grow side by side all year round. Add fresh basil to the mix and the flavors are not only beautifully compatible but, as one friend exclaimed, *insane*! This is the perfect winter recipe to use those fresh-frozen berries tucked away in your freezer, or to make in summer at the height of berry season, using frozen orange juice and zest and the jar of Orange Sugar or Basil Orange Sugar (page 21) you made during the winter. You can also replace 1 cup of the berries with bite-size chunks of orange. All you need to serve is whipped cream or vanilla ice cream.

Preheat oven to 400 degrees F (200 degrees C). Have a 9-inch (23 cm) square glass or Pyrex baking dish ready.

Filling

Place the cherries and blueberries in a large pot or saucepan. Toss in the sugar to coat the berries. Whisk the cornstarch into the orange juice until the mixture is smooth; add to the fruit along with the salt, vanilla, and cider. Stir well. Place over medium heat and bring up to a boil before lowering the heat slightly and allowing the fruit to cook at a simmer for 3 minutes, stirring constantly. Remove from the heat, stir in the basil, and pour into the baking dish.

1 1/2 cups (7 ounces / 200 g)
all-purpose flour

1 tablespoon baking powder

1/4 teaspoon salt

1 orange, finely zested

3 tablespoons Orange Sugar
(page 21) or granulated
white sugar

5 tablespoons (2 1/2 ounces /
75 g) butter, cold but slightly
softened, cubed

1 large egg

1/4 cup (65 ml) milk, plus more if
needed

2 to 3 tablespoons Orange
Sugar or Basil Orange Sugar
(page 21)

Biscuit Topping

Place the flour, baking powder, salt, and zest into a large mixing bowl; whisk or stir to combine, and then add 3 tablespoons Orange Sugar. Add the butter, and using the tips of your fingers, rub it into the flour mixture until it is completely incorporated and resembles cornmeal or damp sand. Whisk the egg into the milk and add to the flour mixture. Lightly stir with a fork just until well-combined and a thick batter forms.

Scoop and drop—do not pack—the dough by very large even spoonfuls over the fruit in 9 dough clusters. Sprinkle 2 to 3 tablespoons of Orange Sugar evenly over the dough and bake for 15–20 minutes until the dough is puffed up, firm, and the tops of the biscuits are golden brown. Remove from the oven to a rack and allow to cool until the fruit juices are no longer bubbling.

Serve warm or at room temperature with freshly whipped, slightly sweetened cream, and a dusting of Orange Sugar, or a scoop of your favorite ice cream.

Orange, Ricotta, and Chèvre Tart in an Orange-Almond Pastry Crust

Makes 1 (9-inch / 23 cm)
round or 1 (13 x 3³/4-inch /
33 x 9 cm) rectangular tart

ORANGE-ALMOND PASTRY
CRUST

1 1/4 cups (6 ounces / 165 g)
    all-purpose flour

1/4 cup (50 g) granulated
    white sugar

1/2 teaspoon baking powder

1/4 cup (1 ounce / 25 g) finely
    ground almonds

1 orange, zested

7 tablespoons (3 1/2 ounces /
    100 g) unsalted butter, cubed

1 large egg, lightly beaten

FRESH GOAT CHEESE, CHÈVRE, A SPECIALTY OF THE AREA of the Loire Valley near Chinon where I live, is found on our hotel breakfast buffet table every morning to be eaten topped with crushed walnuts and locally produced honey. I created this tart when I once found myself with too much goat cheese on my hands. Of course, honey is the perfect sweetener for this mild, slightly tangy cheese, and orange flavors it beautifully.

Ricotta not only adds body to the filling, but it also balances the tang of the goat cheese so it isn't overpowering, giving this tart the taste of cheesecake. Only better. For a more pronounced orange flavor, drizzle a few tablespoons of Orange Syrup (page 144) or warmed marmalade over the top of the baked tart, or spread a thin layer of orange marmalade on the prebaked crust before adding the filling and baking.

Orange-Almond Pastry Crust

Lightly butter a rectangular tart pan, about 13 x 3 3/4 x 1 inches (33 x 9 cm), or a 9-inch (23 cm) round tart pan or plate, preferably with a removable bottom.

Prepare the crust by combining the flour, sugar, baking powder, almonds, and zest in a medium mixing bowl; toss the ingredients together, breaking up any clumps of zest. Using your thumbs and fingertips, rub the butter into the flour until completely incorporated and the consistency of damp sand. Vigorously stir in the egg until all of the dry ingredients are moistened and a dough starts to pull together.

Gather the dough into a ball and place on a lightly floured surface. Using the heel of one hand, smear the dough little by little away from you in quick, hard strokes to blend in any remaining clumps of butter. Scrape up the dough

ORANGE-RICOTTA FILLING

1 cup (8 ounces / 250 g) ricotta cheese, drained

1/2 cup (4 1/2 ounces / 127 g) fresh chèvre, drained

1/4 cup (65 ml) heavy whipping cream

3 to 4 tablespoons honey, divided

3 tablespoons freshly squeezed orange juice

1 teaspoon finely grated orange zest

1/2 teaspoon vanilla extract

1/8 teaspoon salt

1 tablespoon cornstarch

2 large eggs

2 to 3 tablespoons orange marmalade, optional

into a ball, flour the work surface lightly, and knead the dough very briefly and quickly until you have a smooth, homogenous dough. Wrap in plastic wrap and refrigerate until firm enough to roll out, 20–30 minutes.

Once chilled, roll out the dough on a lightly floured work surface to a thickness of about 1/8 inch (scant 1/2 cm) and a little larger than the pan you will be using, making sure to account for the depth of the pan.

Press the dough well into the corners and around the edges of the pan and trim away the excess dough so that it is flush with the edge of the pan. Cover loosely with plastic wrap and chill for 20 minutes.

Preheat the oven to 375 degrees F (190 degrees C). Remove the tart shell from the refrigerator and discard the plastic wrap. Prick the bottom and sides of the shell with a fork, line with aluminum foil or parchment paper, and cover the bottom with pastry weights or dried beans. Bake for 10 minutes; carefully remove from the oven and lift out the foil with the weights. Return the pan to the oven and bake for an additional 3–4 minutes until the bottom of the shell is set and very lightly colored. Remove from the oven.

Reduce oven temperature to 350 degrees F (180 degrees C).

Orange-Ricotta Filling

Place the ricotta, chèvre, cream, 3 tablespoons honey, orange juice, zest, vanilla, and salt in a medium mixing bowl. Sift the cornstarch into the bowl and beat with an electric mixer just to blend. Add the eggs and beat on medium speed until all the ingredients are well-blended and smooth. Taste and add the remaining tablespoon of honey, if desired.

Pour the filling into the tart shell and smooth. Bake until the filling is set in the center and lightly colored, about 30 minutes. Remove from the oven to a cooling rack and allow to cool. Once the tart has cooled to room temperature, place in the refrigerator to chill and set. If your tart pan has a removable bottom, lift out the tart by pushing the bottom up and out from the sides of the pan and carefully sliding the tart off of the pan bottom onto a serving platter; the tart can be served in the tart plate. If you would like, warm the marmalade then drizzle it over the top of the tart before serving.

1 recipe Orange-Almond Pastry
Crust (page 184)

1/2 cup (2 1/2 ounces / 65 g) fresh
pine nuts, lightly toasted

1 cup (3 1/2 ounces / 100 g) finely
ground almonds

8 tablespoons plus 2 teaspoons
(4 1/2 ounces / 125 g) unsalted
butter, softened to room
temperature

3/4 cup (150 g) granulated
white sugar

2 large eggs

2 large egg yolks

1 tablespoon amber rum or
1/2 teaspoon vanilla extract

1 tablespoon plus 2 teaspoons
(1 ounce / 25 g) all-purpose
flour

1 and a scant 1/4 cups
(5 1/2 ounces / 150 g) fresh
pine nuts, lightly toasted,
divided

1 medium-large orange, finely
zested

4 to 5 tablespoons orange
marmalade

Confectioners' sugar, for dusting

La Pinolata

LA PINOLATA, THE PINE NUT TART, IS A TRADITIONAl, homey favorite in Italy; a dense nutty tart baked in a sweet pastry crust. You'll find several variations of the pinolata depending on city and region, with fillings ranging from pastry cream, to a ricotta, to chocolate-based cream, but always containing pine nuts. My own version begins with an orange- and almond-scented sweet pastry crust spread with a thin layer of bittersweet orange marmalade. An almond, rum, and pine nut frangipane is then smoothed atop the marmalade, and then sprinkled with more pine nuts. I find that the tart improves the following day, so don't hesitate to make this the day before serving.

Lightly butter a 9- or 10-inch (23 or 25 cm) round tart pan.

Roll out the prepared dough and carefully fit into the prepared pan, making sure the sides are well-pressed in. Trim the edges level with the top of the pan. Cover with plastic wrap and refrigerate for at least 30 minutes.

Preheat oven to 325 degrees F (180 degrees C).

Place the 1/2 cup (65 g) pine nuts and ground almonds together in a grinder or food processor and whiz for several seconds until both nuts are finely ground and combined.

Place the butter and sugar in a large mixing bowl and beat on medium speed until creamy and smooth. Beat in the eggs, egg yolks, and rum or vanilla extract. Add the ground nuts, flour, 1/3 cup (2 ounces / 50 g) whole pine nuts, and zest and beat on low speed until well-blended.

Remove the tart shell from the refrigerator and spread the marmalade evenly over the bottom in a very thin coating, making sure you spread it up to the edges. Pour or spoon the filling on top of the marmalade and spread, smoothing the top. Sprinkle the remaining whole pine nuts evenly over the top of the filling and gently press onto the filling using the back of a spoon or your fingertips.

Bake for 30–35 minutes, depending on the size of your tart pan and your oven, until the top is slightly puffed and a nice golden color. The filling should be set but with a slight give, indicating it is still moist and not baked dry. The edges of the crust should be golden and cooked. Remove the tart from the oven, place onto a cooling rack, and allow to cool. Serve at room temperature lightly dusted with confectioners' sugar.

Gooseberry Orange Lattice Pie

Makes 1 (10-inch / 25 cm)
deep-dish pie

SWEET PASTRY CRUST FOR
DOUBLE-CRUST PIE

2 1/2 cups (12 ounces / 340 g)
  cake or all-purpose flour

1/2 cup (100 g) granulated
  white sugar

2 oranges, finely zested

14 tablespoons (7 ounces /
  200 g) unsalted butter chilled
  but slightly softened and
  cubed

2 large eggs, lightly beaten

GOOSEBERRY AND ORANGE IS A CLASSIC combination for jam in England, both fruit often paired with ginger as well. I put the three together to create this pie, marrying the bright tartness of red gooseberries, the sweetness of oranges, and the warm, spicy flavor of ginger, all in a cookie-like pastry crust. This pie is best made in advance, allowing enough time to chill in the refrigerator so the filling sets. Delicious served the old-fashioned way, with a scoop of vanilla ice cream.

Sweet Pastry Crust for Double-Crust Pie

Toss the flour, sugar, and zest together in a large mixing bowl until blended and the zest is no longer in clumps. Add the butter, tossing to coat with the dry ingredients. Using thumbs and fingertips, rub the butter into the dry ingredients until completely incorporated and the consistency of damp sand. Vigorously stir in the eggs until all the dry ingredients are moistened and a dough starts to pull together.

Gather the dough together, pressing into a ball and place on a lightly floured surface. Using the heel of one hand, smear the dough little by little away from you in quick, hard strokes in order to make sure that all of the butter is blended in well. Scrape up the dough, lightly flour the surface, and knead very briefly and quickly until you have a smooth, homogeneous dough, adding a bit more flour if needed. Wrap in plastic wrap and refrigerate for 30 minutes.

Roll out half of the chilled dough to fit a 10 x 2-inch (25 x 5 cm) or deeper deep-dish pie pan allowing some overhang and place in the refrigerator. Roll the remaining dough out into a round just larger than the pie pan and cut into even strips.

Preheat the oven to 375 degrees F (190 degrees C).

3 cups (16 ounces / 450 g)
  gooseberries

2 cups (16 ounces / 450 g)
  bite-size orange chunks, about
  3 oranges, drained

4 to 4 1/2 ounces (115 to 125 g)
  diced candied ginger

3/4 cup (150 g) granulated
  white sugar

3 1/2 tablespoons (1 ounce / 35 g)
  cornstarch

1/2 teaspoon ground cinnamon

1 orange, zested

1 tablespoon milk

1 tablespoon Orange Sugar
  (page 21) or granulated
  white sugar

Fruit Filling

Place the gooseberries, orange chunks, and candied ginger into a large mixing bowl. Whisk the sugar, cornstarch, cinnamon, and zest together in a small bowl to combine. Pour the dry ingredients over the fruit and toss until all of the fruit is evenly coated. Remove the pie pan from the refrigerator, pour the fruit into the bottom crust and spread evenly. Weave the dough strips atop the fruit to create a lattice top, allowing each end of the strips to hang over the edge. Pinch the lattice strips to the bottom crust to seal and trim off all excess dough.

Lightly brush the lattice strips with milk and dust generously with Orange Sugar.

Place the pie on a baking sheet and bake for about 50 minutes, or until the crust is golden and cooked and the fruit juices bubbling.

Carefully remove the pie from the oven and place on a cooling rack. Allow to cool completely, as the filling may be very juicy. Chilling the pie in the refrigerator for several hours will help the juices set.

Orange Curd Tartlets in a Coconut Pastry Crust

Makes 8 tartlets or a
9-inch tart

ORANGE CURD

6 large egg yolks, lightly beaten

3/4 cup (150 g) granulated
    white sugar

2 tablespoons cornstarch

1 heaping tablespoon finely
    grated orange zest

3/4 cup (190 ml) freshly squeezed
    orange juice (about 3 juice
    oranges)

8 tablespoons (4 ounces / 120 g)
    unsalted butter, cubed

COCONUT PASTRY CRUST

1 1/4 cups plus 1 tablespoon
    (6 ounces / 170 g) all-purpose
    flour, divided

1/2 teaspoon baking powder

1/8 teaspoon salt

1/3 cup (scant 1 ounce / 28 g)
    dried coconut flakes

7 tablespoons (3 1/2 ounces /
    100 g) unsalted butter,
    softened but cool

3 tablespoons Orange Sugar
    (page 21) or granulated
    white sugar

1 large egg

1 teaspoon finely grated
    orange zest

(continued)

INDIVIDUAL LEMON TARTLETS, LITTLE PASTRY SHELLS filled with tart lemon curd and dressed with a thin slice of lemon poached—just this side of candied—in sugar syrup, is a standard in all French bakeries and pastry shops, and may be one of the country's most popular treats. Here is my flavorful orange version; smooth and creamy, sweet and tart against a simple cookie-like background with a hint of coconut.

Prepare the orange curd the day before or, at the very least, several hours before making the tartlet shells. Prepare the dough the following day and candy the orange slices while the dough is chilling before baking the shells. Assemble the tartlets once all the elements have been prepared and cooled.

Orange Curd

Place the egg yolks in a large heatproof mixing bowl. Place the bowl on a kitchen towel so it will stay in place. Whisk the egg yolks lightly.

In a medium saucepan, stir together the sugar and cornstarch. Whisk in the zest and juice until the sugar and cornstarch are dissolved. Cook over medium-low heat, whisking vigorously, until thickened and just beginning to bubble, about 2 minutes.

Slowly pour the hot orange mixture into the egg yolks in a thin stream while whisking vigorously in order to heat the yolks gradually and gently. Once the hot mixture has been whisked into the yolks, pour and scrape everything back into the saucepan. Cook over medium-low heat, whisking constantly, until it comes to a gentle boil, lowering heat if necessary so it doesn't burn. Continue to cook and whisk for 2 minutes until thickened.

Remove the curd from the heat and whisk in the butter, 1 or 2 cubes at a time, until all the butter is incorporated and the curd is smooth and thick. Scrape into a bowl or large measuring cup, cover with plastic wrap, pressing the wrap directly onto the surface of the curd to keep a skin from forming, and allow to cool to tepid before refrigerating for several hours, or preferably overnight.

(continued)

1 small orange, not more than 8
   ounces (225 g)

3 tablespoons sugar

1 cup (250 ml) water

2 to 3 tablespoons flaked
   coconut, for serving

Coconut Pastry Crust

Stir 1 1/4 cups flour, baking powder, salt, and coconut together in a medium
mixing bowl. In a large mixing bowl, beat the butter and sugar just until
smooth and creamy. Beat in the egg and zest.

Beat in the flour mixture in 2 additions until completely mixed. Turn
dough out onto a work surface floured with 1 tablespoon flour and knead until
the flour is absorbed and a smooth, homogeneous dough, soft but not sticky, is
formed. Wrap in plastic wrap and refrigerate until firm, at least 20–30 minutes.

Lightly butter 8 individual 3 to 3 1/2 x 1-inch (7 1/2 to 8 1/2 cm) round
tartlet tins and place on a baking sheet.

Divide the dough into 8 equal portions and roll each portion into rounds
of no more than a 1/8-inch (1/4 cm) thickness. Line the tins, carefully lifting the
dough and pressing into place, pinching together any tears in the soft dough.
Trim any excess dough above the edges. Chill the tartlet shells while the oven
preheats.

Preheat the oven to 400 degrees F (200 degrees C). Line each shell with
parchment or foil, fill with pastry weights or dried beans, and bake for 6
minutes. Carefully lift out the weights and parchment, and return the shells
to the oven to complete baking for an additional 8–10 minutes until golden
brown. Remove to racks to cool completely.

Candied Orange Slices

A single orange slice will be laid atop the curd in each pastry shell so you want
to make sure the orange you choose for candying is not wider than the inside of
the pastry shell.

Cut the ends off of the orange, about 1/2 to 1 inch (1 to 2 cm), until you
have a nice view of the fruit. Cut the orange into very thin, even slices—you'll
need 8 for the individual tartlets.

Place the sugar and water in a pan wide enough to hold all of the orange slices in 1 layer with room to flip them during the cooking. Bring to a low boil and allow to boil for about 2 minutes until the sugar has dissolved. Slide the orange slices into the liquid. Continue cooking at a simmer for 11–13 minutes, carefully turning the slices every few minutes, until the orange pith and rind is soft and fairly translucent and there is only a thin layer of syrup remaining underneath the oranges. Remove from the heat and allow to completely cool in the pan.

When you are ready to assemble the tartlets, carefully lift the slices from the pan and place on a plate. Drizzle any remaining syrup in the pan over the orange slices.

Tartlets

Pop the pastry shells out of the tins and place on a rack or serving platter. Remove the curd from the refrigerator and beat briefly to loosen and smooth. Divide evenly between the pastry shells and smooth the tops. Top each tartlet with 1 candied orange slice and dust with more coconut, if desired. Serve immediately or keep stored in the refrigerator until ready to serve.

My Dad's Orange Frosty

Makes 2 large or 4 small
drinks

1/2 cup (125 ml) cold milk

1/2 cup (125 ml) cold water

1/3 cup (85 ml) frozen orange
juice concentrate

1/4 cup (50 g) granulated white
sugar

1/2 teaspoon vanilla extract

6 to 8 ice cubes

I MAY HAVE GROWN UP IN ORANGE COUNTRY DRINKING the
most famous, and freshest, orange juice in the world, but my cousins up north
grew up drinking *Orange Julius*; the celebrated frosty beverage made with
orange juice concentrate, sugar, milk, powdered egg whites, and vanilla flavoring
whizzed up in a blender with ice until frothy. This was my dad's version of
that legendary summer drink, one he never tired of making and we never tired
of drinking, winter as well as summer. If you like, replace the cold water and
orange juice concentrate with 1 cup (250 ml) freshly squeezed orange juice and
the finely grated zest of 1 orange. My son would probably throw in a scoop or
two of vanilla ice cream.

Put all of the ingredients in a blender, and starting at the lowest speed and
working up to the highest speed, whiz until the ice is crushed and the drink
is frothy.

Orange Mint Granita

Serves 4

1/2 cup (125 ml) sparkling white wine, Crémant de Loire, or Prosecco

1 1/2 cups (375 ml) freshly squeezed orange juice

3 tablespoons honey, or to taste

1/2 teaspoon freshly squeezed lemon juice

1 sprig (8 to 10 small leaves) fresh mint

ONE OF MY FAVORITE SNACKS WHEN I WAS A KID was frozen fruit juice, and orange topped the list. I would fill small paper cups with orange juice and pop them in the freezer. When I got home from school, biking the distance in the Florida heat, I would grab a teaspoon and one of the paper cups, the juice now frozen solid, and spend a refreshing half hour or so hacking away at the frozen treat with the spoon and scooping up chunks and flakes, letting them melt on my tongue, icy cold and orangey. When I was impatient and couldn't wait the time it took to freeze, the juice would be slush, and that was even better.

This recipe captures that childhood treat and puts an adult twist on it. I discovered that adding sparkling wine, personally preferring a Crémant de Loire, or Prosecco, keeps the orange juice from freezing solid, creating icy, smooth flakes much like the granitas or water ices I would eat all summer long during the years we lived in Italy. The hint of wine and the mint offer a refreshing, adult flourish to this cool treat.

For this recipe, you do not want to use a really sweet sparkling white wine, rather one that is dry and mellow, leaving the orange to flavor and sweeten the mix. I prefer using very sweet juice oranges. You can also use two types of oranges, replacing one of the sweet oranges with a blood orange or two for a slightly altered flavor and a beautiful deepened color.

Whisk the wine, orange juice, honey, and lemon juice together in a large measuring cup until the honey has dissolved and everything is well-blended. Pour the liquid into a metal pan or a plastic container, preferably with a lid. Gently crush the mint leaves between your fingers without breaking or tearing them from the stem and push the sprig into the liquid. Cover the container with a lid or plastic wrap and place in the freezer.

For a shallow pan, stir every 15 minutes or so, until ready to serve. For a deeper container, stir every few hours and then leave in the freezer overnight. The larger and shallower your pan (8 x 12 x 1 inch / 20 x 30 x 2 cm), the quicker the granita will be ready to serve.

Stir before serving and feel free to top with whipped cream and raspberries when in season.

Som Loy Gaeo

Serves 4 to 6

1 1/2 cups (300 g) granulated
  white sugar

3 cups (750 ml) water

2 tablespoons orange blossom
  water

2 1/2 pounds (1 kg) oranges,
  about 5

Crushed ice

A SIMPLE FRUIT TREAT, THIS IS THE PERFECT STREET FOOD eaten in Thailand as a refresher for the muggy, sultry summer afternoons. Prepare the oranges and the syrup in advance, chill them thoroughly, then combine them and top with crushed ice when you are ready to serve. Thais often scent the syrup with jasmine flower water, so I have added fragrant orange blossom water in its place. This traditional Thai street food recipe was shared with me by my friend Nancie McDermott, author of *Real Thai*, *Quick & Easy Thai*, and *Simply Vegetarian Thai Cooking*, an expert on the cuisine of Thailand.

Combine the sugar and water in a medium saucepan and bring to a boil. Lower heat to medium and cook at a low boil, stirring occasionally to dissolve the sugar, until you have a thin, smooth slightly golden syrup, 10–15 minutes. Remove from the heat and cool to room temperature. Stir in the orange blossom water, cover, and refrigerate to chill.

Peel the oranges with a sharp knife removing the top and bottom ends, cutting off the peel and white pith. Cut the oranges into supremes and place in a bowl, adding any runoff juice; cover and refrigerate.

When the supremes and syrup are well-chilled, divide the fruit between individual serving bowls, drizzle each serving with a generous amount of syrup, and top with 2 or 3 tablespoons of crushed ice; serve immediately.

Acknowledgments

A HEARTFELT THANK YOU TO ALL WHO MADE THIS BOOK POSSIBLE:

Martha Hopkins, the best darn agent out there, who believed in me well before my ideas were formed and made me believe in myself, who instructed, guided, and encouraged me, who cheered me on and pushed me to be better at everything I do.

Michelle Branson, my editor, who believed in me as a writer and shared my vision and passion for this project from the very beginning, supported and advised me as she let me go my own way, who allowed me to create a collection of recipes that reflect my home and kitchen and my love for oranges. The excellent, supportive team at Gibbs Smith whose flawless and tireless work made my job easier and so enjoyable, and who produced a stunning book.

Ilva Beretta, incredibly talented photographer, who captured the spirit of my recipes in every stunning image, bringing each dish to life, and who is the best, most supportive friend I have.

All of my friends who enthusiastically and tirelessly tested recipes and gave brilliant feedback, who generously shared their own favorite orange recipes, brainstormed new ideas, and helped me perfect every recipe that went into this book: Deepa and Geetha Gopinath, Ilva Beretta, Elizabeth Morris, Sharon Miro, Catherine Dagneaux, Stacy Livingston Rushton, Isabelle Jezequel, Michelle Hamard, Jill O'Connor, Nancie McDermott, Lynn Gowdy, Joe Seals, Barb Kiebel and Larry Noak, Wendy Austin, Kathy Gold, David Santori, Renee Iseson, Judith Greenwood, Jenni Field, Betsy Cohen, Linda Bain Woods, Valerie Scrivner, Sita Krishnaswamy, Kimberly Nitchkey, Kate McDermott and Kirsten Kubert.

I am forever grateful to my husband Jean-Pierre and our team at the Hôtel Diderot, Nathalie, Ophélie, Françoise, Abeline, and Christelle, who patiently listened to me chatter on endlessly about oranges and the cookbook and who graciously taste tested whatever I brought to them.

And Jean-Pierre, Clément, and Simon, who make everything possible.

Index

JAMIE SCHLER GREW UP IN FLORIDA, surrounded by citrus groves on the stretch of the Space Coast sandwiched between the Atlantic Ocean and the Indian River. She now owns and operates Hôtel Diderot in Chinon, France, and has an award-winning food and lifestyle blog, lifesafeast.net. Schler offers food writing workshops and writes articles for numerous magazines, including *Fine Cooking, The Kitchn, France Magazine, The Art of Eating, Leite's Culinaria,* and *Huffington Post.*

ILVA BERETTA IS A SWEDISH PHOTOGRAPHER based in Tuscany, Italy. She specializes in food and still life photography, and has worked with magazines such as *The Art of Eating, Sale & Pepe, Mat & Vänner,* and *Condé Nast.* She was a finalist in both the Sony World Photography Awards and the Pink Lady Food Photographer of the Year Awards in 2016.

The author and photographer's collaborative website, platedstories.com, won the 2014 IACP Digital Media Award for Best Photo-Based Blog and was a finalist in *Saveur* Magazine's Best Food Blog Awards for Best Writing. Schler's Life's a Feast blog won the 2017 IACP Digital Media Award for the Narrative Culinary Blog category.